"These materials are Bible-b_____ ____ ___ __ ___ believer in an interactive, personal discovery process of God's purposes for fruitful and victorious living."

Dr. John Orme, Executive Director,
Interdenominational Foreign
Mission Association

"Some of the best discipleship materials I have seen. I appreciate the centrality of Scripture and the Christ-centered focus."

Dr. Hans Finzel, Executive Director,
CBInternational

"The power of these books comes from the lifestyle of two people who practice these truths and teach them to others."

Barry St. Clair, Founder and Director,
Reach Out Ministries

"This discipleship curriculum is easy to read and easy to use. I heartily recommend it for [those] who desire to know Christ and make Him known."

Dr. George Murray, President,
Columbia International University,
former General Director of
The Evangelical Alliance Mission (TEAM)

DARING DISCIPLE SERIES

Walking in the Spirit

BILL JONES AND TERRY POWELL

CHRISTIAN PUBLICATIONS, INC.
CAMP HILL, PENNSYLVANIA

CHRISTIAN PUBLICATIONS, INC.
3825 Hartzdale Drive, Camp Hill, PA 17011
www.cpi-horizon.com
www.christianpublications.com

Faithful, biblical publishing since 1883

Walking in the Spirit
ISBN: 0-87509-894-0
LOC Control Number: 2001-130443
© 2001 by Christian Publications, Inc.
All rights reserved

01 02 03 04 05   5 4 3 2 1

For information, write:
Crossover Communications International
Box 211755
Columbia, SC USA 29221

Dedication

To Stephen Franklin Jones
May you be a man of good reputation, full of
the Holy Spirit, full of

- wisdom

- faith

- grace

- and power

(Acts 6:3, 5, 8)

and

To Stephen Floyd Powell
The name "Stephen" stems from Greek,
and means "crown of victory."
May you always tap into the Holy Spirit's power
and live a victorious Christian Life.

CONTENTS

Introduction 1

CHAPTER ONE:
Who Is the Holy Spirit? 3

CHAPTER TWO:
What Does the Holy Spirit Do? (Part 1) 15

CHAPTER THREE:
What Does the Holy Spirit Do? (Part 2) 27

CHAPTER FOUR:
Why Am I Not Experiencing the
Holy Spirit's Power? 39

CHAPTER FIVE:
How Do I Grieve the Holy Spirit? 55

CHAPTER SIX:
How Do I Quench the Holy Spirit? 69

CHAPTER SEVEN:
What Does It Mean to Be "Filled with
the Holy Spirit"? 85

CHAPTER EIGHT:
How Can I Be Filled with the Holy Spirit? 99

CHAPTER NINE:
How Can I Walk in the Holy Spirit? 113

CHAPTER TEN:

How Can I Exhibit the Fruit
of the Holy Spirit? 131

CHAPTER ELEVEN:

How Do I Demonstrate the Gifts of the
Holy Spirit?...155

CHAPTER TWELVE:

How Do I Demonstrate the Power of the
Holy Spirit?...165

APPENDIX A:

Spiritual Gifts Test 177

APPENDIX B:

The Question of "Speaking in Tongues".....193

APPENDIX C:

The One-Verse Method—John 3:16..........199

Endnotes..211
Memory Verses 217

Introduction

Walking in the Spirit is a Bible study guide for your individual benefit. Yet this discipleship material will have maximum profit for you if you're a part of a group that meets on a weekly basis. A *Leader's Guide* for *Walking in the Spirit* is available from the publisher.

Other titles in the Daring Disciple Series include:

> *Knowing God*
> *Discovering Your Identity*
> *Learning to Trust*

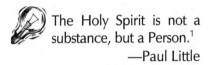 The Holy Spirit is not a substance, but a Person.[1]
—Paul Little

CHAPTER ONE

Who Is the Holy Spirit?

Have you ever "jumped" a dead car battery? When the temperature plummets or you leave the headlights on, the battery may get too weak to spark the engine. In that case you would need to recruit another driver to pull his car alongside yours. Utilizing jumper cables to connect your weaker battery to his stronger one, the juice flows from the functional battery through the cables into your depleted battery. With the fresh infusion of power, your engine starts and you're on your way.

What a picture of the Holy Spirit's ministry! Jesus called Him the "Comforter" (LB) or "Helper" (John 14:26). The term Jesus used to describe the Holy Spirit actually means "One who comes alongside" to provide assistance. Just think: when our spiritual batteries get weak—when we need an infusion of power for Christian living or ministry—there's Someone to give us the "jump" we need!

This discipleship course is all about the Holy Spirit: who He is, what He does and why so few Christians experience His power. Through your studies you will find out what it means to be "filled with the Spirit." You will identify ways we grieve the Holy Spirit, the characteristics of a person who is yielded to Him and the various ways He empowers us to accomplish God's work in the world.

This initial chapter addresses the most fundamental question of all: *Who is the Holy Spirit?* So pop your hood and get out your jumper cables. (Unless you already possess all the spiritual energy you need, that is.)

Comparison to Humanity

Imagine you're from the central part of the United States, and during your vacation, you see the Pacific Ocean for the first time. You're overwhelmed by its vastness. You think of several friends back home who have never seen an ocean, and you wish they could share the experience with you. Then an idea pops into your head; you get a jar, scoop it full of ocean water and take it back to show your friends. "Now they can see the ocean too," you reason.

Of course, having a jar of ocean water substitute for a view of the ocean is inadequate to say the least. That reminds us of the futility in tackling the question, "Who is the Holy Spirit?" in just a few pages. The result may be far from adequate. Yet God's Word does reveal information that's relevant to the question.

The most fundamental truth Scripture discloses is that *the Holy Spirit is a Person*—not a substance, nor an impersonal force. Too often even believers refer to Him with the impersonal term "it," instead of the pronoun "He." His personhood becomes clear when you examine ways the Holy Spirit compares to both human and divine personality traits.

The human personality consists of three parts: mind, will and emotion. Our mind enables us to think on a level that far surpasses other species in the animal kingdom. We can reason and experience what's called self-consciousness as we proceed through the day. Our will is a God-given capacity to choose. Instead of being the robotic products of our environment we can choose how to respond to people and to circumstances. Our emotional nature ensures that we exhibit a wide variety of feelings or affections. We experience life with our heart, not just with our head.

The Holy Spirit also exhibits these three facets of personality: *mind, will* and *emotion.* Look up the Bible verses that follow.

Q **Which facet of personality does each reference mention?**

A Romans 15:30 *love — emotion*

A First Corinthians 2:11 *thoughts — mind*

A First Corinthians 12:11 *determines — will*

To discern the thoughts of God the Father, the Holy Spirit exercises intellect (mind). Decisions regarding the distribution of spiritual gifts to believers involve His will. His love for us necessarily involves His affections, or emotions.

We can also treat, or respond to, the Holy Spirit as we do other people.

Q Consult the following verses and record the various ways people treat Him.

A Acts 5:3 _lie, deceive_

A Acts 7:51 _resist_

A Acts 10:19-21 _obey direction_

A Ephesians 4:30 _grieve_

A First Thessalonians 5:19 _quench "the fire" of_

A Hebrews 10:29 _insult_

What's the rationale for these observation exercises? To rivet deeply into your consciousness the Personhood of the Holy Spirit. Knowing that He is a Person will alter the way you respond to Him. You will be more apt to consider how your conduct affects Him and to tap into His strength for daily living.

Characteristics of Divinity

The personality of the Holy Spirit includes His divine characteristics as well as His human traits. Just as God the Father is a person, so the Holy Spirit is a person with the distinguishing marks of divinity. You often see or hear Him referred to as "God the Spirit."

Q Read Job 33:4. **What does the Holy Spirit's role in creation say about Him?**

A *He is almighty creator, source of life – omnipotent*

Q Digest Psalm 139:7-10. **What does the figurative language in these verses teach us about the Holy Spirit?**

A *He is ever present – omnipresent*

Q Mull over First Corinthians 2:10-12. **What does the Spirit's ability to discern the mind of God the Father say about Him?**

A *He knows all things — omniscient*

Q According to Hebrews 9:14, a divine attribute ascribed to the Holy Spirit is:

A *Source of salvation — holy, sacrificial, saving sanctifying*

The passages you examined disclose four basic qualities that distinguish God the Spirit from human beings. He is all-powerful, or *omnipotent*, as illustrated in the creation of mankind (Job 33:4). He is not limited by space—He is able to be in every place at once. Seen in Psalm 139:7-10, this capacity is called *omnipresence*. There isn't anything the Holy Spirit doesn't know, including the mind of God the Father (1 Corinthians 2:10-12). That's called *omniscience*. From Hebrews 9:14 we add to these divine traits His eternal nature. Every human being began life at a specific point in time. God, however, never had a beginning—He has always existed and He always will.

Functions of Divinity

Not only does the Holy Spirit possess divine attributes, but He has also performed works that only God can do.

Q According to the Bible passages that follow, in what activities unique to God was the Holy Spirit engaged?

A Genesis 1:1-2 *Creation*

A Luke 1:35 *Conception of Christ*

A John 16:8-11 *Conviction of sin, righteousness, and judgment*

A Second Peter 1:20-21 *Prophecy and inspiration of scripture*

God has given man the capacity to create, but raw materials from which to make something new are needed. Not so with God. The universe was created out of nothing and the Holy Spirit was involved (Genesis 1:1-2). Scientists can clone sheep and monkeys but that's a far cry from creating the original genetic material from matter that didn't exist beforehand!

Human beings have penned reams of inspirational stories and poems, but the writing of Scripture required the extraordinary guidance of the Holy Spirit's inspiration (2 Peter 1:20-21). He controlled the thoughts of the human authors so that

every word they wrote was what God intended and
every fact or point they recorded was without error.

Every human birth is a God ordained means of
populating the earth. He designed the entire process
of human and animal procreation. Yet the conception of Jesus Christ, which involved the work of the
Holy Spirit (Luke 1:35), was indeed a *super*natural
act. That Mary conceived while a virgin reveals miraculous power that only God possesses.

Though God uses human agents to communicate
His plan of salvation, only His Spirit can create re-
ceptivity in the heart of a non-Christian. His work
of conviction in the human heart (John 16:8-11) is
solely a divine function. Human evangelists and
teachers of the Bible can only reach the ears of lis-
teners, but the Holy Spirit shuttles the seed of God's
Word to people's hearts where it can take root and
grow.

Three in One

Determining who the Holy Spirit is necessarily
involves discussion of a concept called the "Trinity." It is a difficult concept to grasp because it involves ideas and categories which the finite mental
powers of man cannot fully comprehend. It is a divine reality that human language cannot adequately
describe.

Here's a simplified version of what scholars say on
the subject. God is one being, but He exists in three
persons: God the Father, God the Son (Jesus Christ)
and God the Holy Spirit. According to Paul Little,

There are three modes or forms in which the divine essence exists. "Person" is an imperfect expression of this truth, inasmuch as the term denotes to us a *separate* rational and moral individual. But in the being of God there are not three *individuals*, but only three *personal self distinctions* within the one divine essence. . . . The divine essence is not divided into three: it is fully present in each of the three Persons.[2]

The concept of "Tri-Unity" does *not* mean that Christianity has three Gods. According to Deuteronomy 6:4, "The LORD is our God, the LORD is one!" Yet Scripture clearly indicates that He reveals Himself in three forms. Genesis 1:26 uses a plural pronoun in reference to God's creation: "Let *Us* make man in *Our* image . . ." (emphasis added). The plural pronoun is also seen in the Lord's commissioning of Isaiah: "Whom shall I send, and who will go for *Us*?" (Isaiah 6:8, emphasis added). The New Testament gets more specific by naming each member of the Trinity. In His mandate called "The Great Commission," Jesus referred to the Father, Son and Holy Spirit (Matthew 28:19). After the Spirit (in the form of a dove) descended upon Jesus after His baptism, God the Father spoke a word of commendation to His "beloved Son" (3:17). Jesus informed His disciples of the future ministry of the Holy Spirit on their behalf (John 14:26). And Peter mentioned all three members of the Trinity by name (1 Peter 1:2).

Analogies can often enhance our understanding of the Trinity. The idea of "one person, three roles" is captured in a man who is a son to his parents, a husband to his wife and a father to his children. Another analogy used to depict the Trinity is the three states of water (H_2O). Water may exist in solid form (ice), as a vapor (steam) and as a liquid. Each of the three forms has all of the inherent qualities of water, yet the water exists in three distinct states. Also consider the three dimensions of space: width, length and height. Each is a part of the other, so there is unity, but in a sense each is distinct from the others, which results in a trinity.

Q Which analogy is most helpful to you in explaining God's "three-in-oneness"? Why?

A son, husband, father — The role orientation implies dynamic relationship, practical application

Q If you summarized the content of Chapter 1 in fifty words or less, how would it read? Write your restatement below:

A The Holy Spirit is a person with a mind, will, and emotions. He is also omnipotent, omniscient, and omnipresence. As an aspect of the tri-unity of God, He participated in Creation, salvation, and sanctification of humankind.

Memorizing Scripture

Before your study group meets, commit _John 14:16-17_ to memory. This is Jesus' announcement that the Holy Spirit would serve as the disciples' Helper.

"And I will ask the Father, and He will give you another Counselor to be with you forever — the Spirit of truth. The world cannot accept Him because it neither sees or knows Him. But you know Him, for He lives with you and will be in you."

Too common is the sin of forgetting the Holy Spirit. . . . All His works are good in the most eminent degree: He suggests good thoughts, prompts good actions, reveals good truths, applies good promises, assists in good attainments and leads to good results. There is no spiritual good in all the world of which He is not the author and sustainer.[1]

CHAPTER
TWO

What Does the Holy Spirit Do? (Part 1)

Near a section of highway that's being built or repaired, you may see a sign that reads, CAUTION: CONSTRUCTION WORK AHEAD. Perhaps every believer should wear a similar sign around his neck: CAUTION: CHRISTIAN UNDER CONSTRUCTION.

You are a construction project for the Holy Spirit, who wants to see you grow in character and serve the Lord effectively. His basic job description is to work in you and for you. Some things He has already accomplished for you, other things you are in the process of experiencing.

This chapter examines past works of the Holy Spirit on behalf of believers. You'll discover five ways in which He has already worked in you—since the very moment you became part of the family of

God. These works help explain your privileged position before God. The next chapter will focus on ways in which He serves you in the here and now. His current ministries are called "experiential" works. Becoming aware of what He has done and is willing to do for you may accelerate the completion of His construction project in your life.

Past Performances

When you entered into a personal relationship with Christ, the Holy Spirit became very busy in your life. Look up the following Bible verses.

Q Jot down the words/phrases from the following verses that capture the Holy Spirit's activity on your behalf. (Don't fret if some of the terminology is foreign to you. We'll clarify their meanings in the following pages.)

A 1. First Corinthians 3:16 *God's spirit lives in you*

A 2. First Corinthians 12:13 *God's spirit baptized us into one Body, (quenches spirit thirst) given on Spirit to drink)*

A 3. Second Corinthians 1:22; Ephesians 1:14 *set his seal of ownership on us, as a deposit guaranteeing what is to come*

A 4. Ephesians 1:13 *marked in him with a seal, the promised Holy Spirit*

A 5. Titus 3:5 *washing and renewal by the Holy Spirit — part of salvation and mercy and grace*

Now we will dissect the phrases you recorded to enhance your understanding of the Holy Spirit's activity.

He Regenerates Your Spirit

In Titus 3:5, Paul used the following terminology to describe what happened at conversion: "He saved [you] . . . by the washing of regeneration and renewing by the Holy Spirit." The word *regeneration* comes from two Greek terms that mean "birth again" or "born again." So the initial work of God's Spirit was to regenerate your human spirit and breathe new life into you that made saving faith possible.

> Regeneration is the work of the Holy Spirit upon those who are spiritually dead (see Ephesians 2:1-10). The Spirit recreates the human heart, quickening it from spiritual death to spiritual life. Regenerate people are new creations. Where formerly they had no disposition, inclination, or desire for the things of God, now they are disposed and inclined toward God. In regeneration, God plants a desire for Himself in the human heart that otherwise wouldn't be there. . . . It occurs by God's divine initiative and is an act that is sovereign, immediate, and instantaneous, . . .[2]

Go back and underline the words/phrases from the quotation on page 17 that clarify the truth of regeneration for you.

Q What is significant about the fact that regeneration requires divine rather than human initiative?

A *It is not dependent on human activity, cannot be earned. It is a gift iniated by God.*

Q What is a logical response on your part to God's initiative and the regenerating work of the Holy Spirit?

A *"Why?" and "How?"*

He Indwells Your Body

Old Testament references to the Holy Spirit describe Him as coming *upon* someone for a special purpose and at a specific point in time. For instance, "the Spirit of the LORD came upon Gideon" (Judges 6:34), enabling him to overcome extreme odds to defeat the Midianites. The phrase "the Spirit of the Lord came mightily upon him" (14:6, LB) accounted for Samson's extraordinary strength. But notice that during His earthly ministry, Jesus said the Holy Spirit would be *with* His followers. Jesus described the Spirit as a Helper who would be *with*

His disciples forever and who abides *with* them (John 14:16-17).

After Jesus' ascension into heaven, however, the Bible uses a different preposition in reference to the Holy Spirit. The body of a believer is called a "temple," which serves as a dwelling place for God's Spirit: "Do you not know that you are a temple of God, and that the Spirit of God dwells *in* you?" (1 Corinthians 3:16, emphasis added).

Q Read First Corinthians 6:16-20. **The Holy Spirit resides within us. What is the significance of that truth for *your* daily life?**

A *I need to live as one who is united to the Lord as two become one in act of sex*

Now digest the implications cited by two renowned leaders of Christianity. Billy Graham said, "If we realized that God Himself in the person of the Holy Spirit really dwells within our bodies, we would be far more careful about what we eat, drink, look at or read."[3] Watchman Nee put an exclamation point to Graham's statement: "When we really see that God has made our hearts His dwelling place, what a deep reverence will come over our lives! All lightness, all frivolity will end."[4]

Q Respond to this question: **If I had lived the past twenty-four hours with a keen awareness of the Holy Spirit's presence within, what would I have done differently?**

A I would have been more controlled in speaking to Linda, Robert, and Bob. I may not have watched "the other sister" because it

Talk over your answer with the Lord. Confess any sin that you identified and ask Him for a keener awareness of His presence within you.

triggered my grief, discouragement

He Seals Your Future *over my marriage.*

In Ephesians 1:13 you encountered the following truth: " . . . having also believed, you were *sealed* in Him with the Holy Spirit of promise" (emphasis added).

In Paul's era, a seal was a mark of ownership. To identify or set apart an item, an individual or a business would put a particular seal on it so everyone would know who owned it. Whoever shipped a box of chariot wheels from Jerusalem to Athens would put his seal on the shipment. Whoever received it would note the seal and know who sent it. The seal of ownership was similar to the brands used by cattle ranchers—every rancher uses a different brand, signifying ownership. When you were converted to Christ, God put His "seal" on you to represent the fact that you belong to Him.

logo

Read First Corinthians 6:19-20 again. **How does it make you feel to know that "you are not your own"? Why?**

A *Loved, free and focused. awed and responsible To serve the Lord*

Q Paul emphasized that "you have been bought with a price" (6:20). **What price did God pay in order to make you His property?**

A *The death of Jesus Christ on cross – Sacrificial Lamb of God*

Q You've learned that God's Spirit has marked you as God's property. **How should knowing this affect your attitude or emotional state?**

A *Joyful, secure, purposeful*

Being sealed by the Holy Spirit provides a believer with an *assurance of salvation.* You can be sure that God will protect His property and eventually bring you safely to heaven. A Bible teacher comments on this issue of assurance: "Figuratively, the seal indicates that we are children of God and belong to Him and that His Holy Spirit will keep us eternally in God's protective custody, secure from Satan, sin and judgment."[5]

Yet you may experience periods in your life when you don't *feel* secure in the Lord. But the seal of the Holy Spirit represents a benefit, or position before God, that is yours no matter how

you feel. Emotions are subjective and unreliable;
the seal of God's Spirit is <u>an objective reality</u> that
exists for believers apart from your perception of
it. According to Romans 8:38-39, " . . . neither
death, nor life, nor angels, nor principalities, nor
things present, nor things to come, nor powers,
nor height, nor depth, nor any other created
thing, shall be able to separate us from the love of
God, which is in Christ Jesus our Lord."

Here's another author's "bottom line" concerning this doctrine: "<u>The presence of the Holy Spirit is
a spiritual reminder of God's promise to finish what
He has begun in you. It is a sign to the spirit world
that you belong to someone else.</u>"[6]

He Guarantees Your Inheritance

In the same sentence in which Paul referred to
the Holy Spirit's *sealing* of believers, he added
that the Spirit "is given as a *pledge* of our inheritance" (Ephesians 1:14, emphasis added). In a letter to another church, Paul said that God "gave us
the Spirit in our hearts as a *pledge*" (2 Corinthians
1:22, emphasis added).

In these verses Paul uses a term common to the
business world of the first century. <u>A *pledge* served
as a down payment of money to close a business
deal.</u> For example, in Paul's time, to purchase a
donkey a buyer gave the owner partial payment to
indicate that both the buyer and owner had agreed
on a total price for that particular animal. The cur-
rency used in the down payment was called "*earnest*

money." The pledge, or earnest money, told the owner that the buyer intended to follow through on the purchase.

When the Holy Spirit began indwelling you at the moment of conversion, He served as a guarantee that the spiritual transaction, the "product" God purchased on the cross—*you*—would be His forever. Put simply, it was an *obligation to buy*. When the Holy Spirit entered you at the moment of conversion, His presence served as God's down payment or promise to redeem you.

A pledge not only protected the owner in a business transaction, but it also protected the buyer. A down payment on the donkey guaranteed that no one else could purchase the animal out from under the buyer. Similarly, the Holy Spirit's presence in your life at conversion was a guarantee to God the Father that the "product" purchased on the cross—*you*—would be His forever.

A pledge, or earnest money, also represented a sample of what was to come in a business deal. Partial payment for the donkey was a sample of what the buyer would give in the future—more money. In a similar way, the Holy Spirit is a sample, or a foretaste, of what you'll receive from God in the future. The most gratifying aspect of your current relationship with the Lord is just a fraction of the joy and benefits that await you.

Bill Bright puts it this way:

By the very presence of the indwelling Holy
Spirit in our lives, we are given a preview of the
inheritance which awaits us in heaven. God . . . is
giving His promise in the form of a "down payment" that our inheritance is real and waiting.[7]

The business analogy we used to explain the concept of "pledge" has several different facets or par-
allels.

Q Which aspect of the analogy means the most
to you? Why?

A *"pledge" of future. My health
issues, having faced cancer
this past summer, griefs
and losses in past five years.*

He Records Your Membership

The term "church" means "a called out assem-
bly," referring to persons whom God has "called
out" from the world and saved through Christ's
work on the cross. The moment you received Christ
you were granted membership in what's called the
universal Church. The universal Church includes all
true believers in every location—those still living as
well as those who have died. An analogy Paul used
frequently to describe the universal Church is "the
body of Christ." Every person whom the Lord has
ever saved is part of Christ's body.

The concepts of the universal Church and the
body of Christ shed light on the work of the Holy
Spirit mentioned in First Corinthians 12:13: *"By
one Spirit we were* all *baptized into one body . . ."*
(emphasis added).

Don't confuse the phrase "baptized into one body" with the popular teaching known as the "second blessing." Some Christians equate the phrase "baptism of the Holy Spirit" with a special experience that they believe follows salvation, a type of "second blessing" accompanied by speaking in tongues and extraordinary power in ministry. *What Paul referred to in First Corinthians 12:13 is a "baptism" that all converts to Christ necessarily experience, not a future event reserved for elite believers.* He employed the metaphor of baptism to represent your official placement into the body of Christ. One commentator describes this as "that divine operation of God's Spirit which places the believer in Christ, in His mystical body, the Church, and which makes him one with all other believers in Christ."[8]

Personal Reflections

The five past works of the Holy Spirit—regenerating your spirit, indwelling your body, sealing your future, guaranteeing your inheritance and recording your membership—help you understand and appreciate your position, or standing, before God and in relation to other Christians.

Q Which work of the Holy Spirit aroused the most gratitude within you? Why?

A *Regeneration. without Christ my life would be nothing, and I would be an emotionally and spiritual disaster.*

Q Which truth do you find most convicting? Why?

A *endwelling your body. I do not take care of myself physically mentally, emotionally very well.*

Q Why do you think God recorded these works of the Holy Spirit in His Word?

A *So we would know in our minds the comprehesivenes of His love, grace and salvation for us... then our emotions and actions can find focus in Him.*

Memorizing Scripture

John 7:37-39 emphasizes that the Holy Spirit quenches our spiritual thirst. Be ready to recite these verses when your study group meets. Verse 37 refers to the second half of the verse, so start with the words, "If any man is thirsty. . . ." Verse 39 includes only the first point in the verse, so end with the phrase, "whom those who believed in Him were to receive."

"If anyone is thirsty, let him come to me and drink. Whoever believes in me as the scripture has said, stream of living water will flow from within him. By this He meant the Spirit, whose those who believed in Him were later to recieve."

Trying to live the Christian life in our own strength is like relying on a V-8 engine which has four burnt cylinders. We merely sputter along.

CHAPTER THREE

What Does the Holy Spirit Do? (Part 2)

Thousands came to Christ through this man's global evangelistic ministry. A well-known Bible institute bears his name. Yet from a human perspective, he was an unlikely candidate for public ministry. He had only a few years of formal schooling. Even as an adult, his spelling was abominable. After a crusade he led in England, a journalist wrote, "he butchers the King's English!" He was obese. Folks didn't flock to his meetings because of the magnetic pull of his handsome physical features. The same journalist who criticized his grammar reached the following conclusion after hearing him preach. "I can find no natural explanation for his success." When Dwight L. Moody read the reporter's column, he concurred. "He's right. There is no *natural* explanation."[1]

Dwight L. Moody's life demonstrates that the work of the Holy Spirit isn't all past tense in a believer's life. Just as God's Spirit helped Moody throughout his life, He wants to work for you on a daily basis. The last

chapter examined what the Holy Spirit did for you at
the time of your conversion to Christ. This chapter
shifts to the present tense. You'll <u>identify experiential</u>
<u>works of the Holy Spirit—things He can do for you in</u>
<u>the here and now.</u>

Present Potential

After you read each reference, write your answer to this question:

Q **What is the Holy Spirit able and willing to do
for me now?** (Record key words and phrases.
Later, you'll receive information that deepens
your understanding of these activities.)

A Romans 8:16 *testifies with our
Spirit that we are God's
children*

A First Corinthians 2:9-12 *reveal God's
thoughts to us, even the deep
things of God*

A John 14:16 *Counsels*

A Romans 8:26-27 *helps in weakness,
intercedes for us according to
God's will, searches our hearts*

A Acts 1:8; Romans 8:12-13 *power to
witness, power to put to death
the misdeeds of the body*

He Assures Your Heart

Refer back to Romans 8:16. The point of this passage is that the Holy Spirit provides assurance that your salvation experience was genuine. This is an inward, subjective work of overcoming doubts that are all too typical in Christian experience. When the feelings of a child of God fluctuate, the Spirit reminds him that he has a relationship with Christ, referring him to biblical promises about forgiveness of sin and telling him that God's Word is more reliable than feelings.

This cultivation of assurance works in tandem with other, more objective confirmations. For instance, First John 2:3-4 asserts, "By this we know that we have come to know Him, if we keep His commandments. The one who says, 'I have come to know Him,' and does not keep His commandments, is a liar, and the truth is not in him."

It's obvious John isn't referring to perfect obedience—no one obeys or exhibits marks of newness to a perfect degree. However, he is saying that salvation will make a gradual, qualitative difference in our lifestyle. Seeing even small changes will provide needed assurance. The Holy Spirit doesn't work subjectively to instill assurance unless there is some degree of corresponding objective evidence.

This ministry of assurance is needed most when a Christian sins. Though God's Spirit has moved in, providing a new desire and power to obey the Lord, He doesn't wipe out our sinful nature (see 1 John 1:8). The old sinful bent and the new nature coexist, each vying for control. So subsequent failures may plant doubts about our status before God. When we fail the Lord, instead of questioning the reality of our salvation, we can follow the biblical mandate for handling sin.

Q Read First John 1:8-9. When we're conscious of failing God, what should we do?

A *Confess to God our failings in light of Gods truth*

Q What does He promise to do?

A *He will forgive us and purify us from all unrighteousness*

I (Terry) recall a time as a young boy when my dad made me a homemade kite. He got it off the ground, and a stiff breeze lifted it so high into the sky that I couldn't see it. Then my dad handed me the string and let me hold it. I couldn't see the kite, but I knew it was up there—I could feel it tugging on the string.

When the Holy Spirit assures your heart, you feel His tug.

He Helps You Understand the Bible

"Aha! I've got it!"

"That's it! *Now* I understand!"

We use expressions like these whenever a bright idea pops into our head or when the fuzz in our mind clears and a solution to a problem suddenly appears. You have probably seen the symbol of a turned on lightbulb representing this event in the mind. The bulb conveys the idea of a truth or solution suddenly flashing on, providing light to an otherwise darkened mind.

The word that describes this experience is *illumination*. That term carries the idea of clarifying something or providing light which enhances one's understanding of a concept. We use the term *illumination* to explain an important truth about the relationship of a reader to the Bible. We can understand and think of life areas in which we need to apply its teaching because the Holy Spirit *illuminates* our minds; He turns on the lightbulb in our minds and causes Bible content to come alive for us; He sheds light on passages that otherwise leave us in the dark.

This present, ongoing role of the Holy Spirit is revealed in First Corinthians 2:9-12. The passage says that a non-Christian has a harder time understanding Scripture than a Christian does. That's because an unbeliever doesn't have the Holy Spirit inside him "turning on the light" and giving discernment as he reads.

Q Meditate on the words in Psalm 119:18. **What is one application of realizing our need for the Spirit's illumination?**

A So we can see the wonderful things God has there for us.

To get home one day from a ministry trip, Bill had to fly in a small, four-seater airplane. Since a thunderstorm had delayed them, they did not make it back until very late, requiring them to land the plane in the dark. When the pilot said they were approaching the airport, Bill looked down to find the runway and saw nothing. All the lights had been turned off! Bill asked the pilot (a bit anxiously) if he could land the plane in the dark to which the pilot answered he could *not*. Trying to sound as calm as possible Bill asked if the plane had enough gas to circle the airport until daylight. Sensing his growing concern, the pilot told Bill to look down below. As they flew over the airport the pilot turned the radio knob three times. Instantly, the lights went on and the landing field became visible.

To understand spiritual truth, the Holy Spirit must turn on the lights. Only He can give supernatural understanding of the Scriptures. Next time, before reading the Scriptures, you may want to "turn on the lights" by praying Psalm 119:18 back to the Lord. God's Spirit won't turn you into a scholar, but if you pray for understanding and spend adequate time meditating on the verses, He'll disclose life-changing truth.

He Comforts Your Emotions

Jesus used the term "Helper" to describe the Holy Spirit (John 14:16; 16:7). The term is the noun form of the Greek verb "to encourage." It's a

Greek word that literally means "one who comes alongside." "Comforter" or "encourager" are other apt translations.

The Holy Spirit's comfort is needed because we live in a broken world. Knowing Christ doesn't erase pain and discouragement: people you love still die; your company may still eliminate your job; your teenager may rebel in spite of your positive example. Scripture suggests that joy and pain often coexist. God's Spirit can comfort you by providing an eternal perspective to trials. The support of other Christians may be a conduit through which His power flows. He may soothe you or galvanize your spirit through a truth or promise from the Bible. Whatever means He uses, you can experience "the peace of God, which surpasses all comprehension" (Philippians 4:7).

Q Think of a time in your Christian pilgrimage when you experienced the Holy Spirit's comfort. Briefly describe the experience:

A *teaching innu city, Dad's death, rejection of my husband and our marriage, first RA attack*

Q How can the Holy Spirit's ministry of comfort strengthen your witness to unbelievers whom you know?

A *Sharing with unbelievers the experience of the Holy Spirit's comfort in those decisions*

Nowhere in Scripture does God promise us that the Christian life will be a bed of roses. He does, however, promise us that His Spirit will be with us to comfort, strengthen and encourage us. Instead of taking you *around* difficult times, the Holy Spirit will enable you to go *through* the hard times—triumphantly. Even when you don't know what or how to pray, pray anyway. Simply make yourself available to God. The Holy Spirit will do the rest. He will take your heart's burden to the throne of grace and represent you before your heavenly Father.

He Intercedes for You

Do you ever feel so overwhelmed by a problem, so burdened about a person or circumstance, that you can't even pray clearly? You approach the Lord with the need, yet you fumble, searching for the right words. Your attempt to describe your emotions is muddled. Or perhaps you lack the wisdom to know what to ask for. All you know is that you're hurting and you want to broach the matter with God.

That's when the Holy Spirit takes over. When you're not sure what to say or how to pray, He communicates your innermost thoughts and feelings to God the Father. "The Spirit also helps our weakness; for we do not know how to pray as we should, but the Spirit Himself intercedes for us with groanings too deep for words" (Romans 8:26).

At some point in the future during a time of prayer you will feel frustrated trying to express your feelings or confused about what to ask for.

Q During these times, how will remembering the truth in Romans 8:26-27 encourage you?

A *God understands, hears, and is listening with heart full of love, grace, and wisdom in spite of my helplessness*

He Guides You

Jesus informed His disciples that the Holy Spirit "will *guide* you into all the truth" (John 16:13, emphasis added). This promise had a distinctive meaning to those early disciples. As their futures unfolded, God's Spirit would remind them of things Jesus had said while on earth (14:26). Yet the Bible's promise of divine guidance into truth, as well as wisdom for choices, extends beyond those early disciples to those of us alive today. When allowed, the Holy Spirit plays an active role in the realm of daily decision making.

Q What decisions are looming on the horizon for you right now?

A *How to handle finances and manage my time and health; how to respond to Bob everyday*

Take a few minutes and ask the Lord for guidance. Tell Him that you want the Holy Spirit's perspective to permeate your thinking.

He Empowers Your Life and Ministry

When it comes to holiness, God equips you for what He calls you to do, and who He calls you to be. It is "the law of the Spirit of life" that frees you from the law of sin (Romans 8:2). You overcome temptation "according to the Spirit" (8:4). It is the same Spirit who raised Jesus from the dead who removes the burden of sin's control (8:11).

Revel in the fact that you are neither left alone in your quest for character nor in your efforts to serve the Lord. After Jesus delivered a mandate to evangelize and teach, He pledged His presence "even to the end of the age" (Matthew 28:20). Before He ascended into heaven, He defined that presence as the Holy Spirit who would empower them for ministry (Acts 1:8). Bask in the awareness that ministry is *not* merely a human endeavor.

Q Ponder Paul's reference to his ministry in Colossians 1:28-29. **What words from the text show that he depended on the Holy Spirit for effectiveness?**

A *"struggling with all his energy which so mightily powerfully works in me."*

As he took a walk one day, A.J. Gordon saw from a distance what looked like a man pumping furiously on an old hand pump. Gordon stared at the man as he continued the feverish activity. The man seemed tireless, pumping up and down without a break, his pace never slowing. Gordon was so captivated he edged closer to the pump. Then he realized that the "man" was actually a life-size wooden figure. The "arm" that appeared to be working so hard was hinged at the elbow, with the "hand" wired to the pump handle. Water gushed from the pump. But the wooden figure wasn't pumping the water. . . . It was rigged so the water was pumping the man![2]

Remember that story when you spot someone who is active for God. The results you see aren't primarily the fruit of human labor: the Holy Spirit is working through that person. *The Holy Spirit is the power behind the pump. All the servant has to do is keep his hand on the handle.*

Personal Reflections

Q Which of the six ministries of the Holy Spirit covered in this chapter (He assures your heart, helps you understand the Bible, comforts your emotions, intercedes for you, guides you and empowers your life and ministry) has been most prevalent in your life since conversion? Explain.

A I have experienced all of them but the Holy Spirit's illumination of God's word and His guidence and empowerment have dominated my spiritual journey.

Q Which present work of the Holy Spirit do you need to experience more often? Explain.

A *Comfort my emotions and intercede for me because of my health issues and my lack of marital relationship or support*

Q Why is it helpful to be aware of these potential ministries of the Holy Spirit?

A *When I need or someone I meet needs any of these, I can share and pray with them more effectively*

Memorizing Scripture

Work on memorizing Luke 4:1, 14. These verses describe the Holy Spirit's work in God the Son prior to and immediately following His wilderness temptations.

"Jesus, full of the Holy Spirit, returned from the Jordan, and was led by the Spirit in the desert."

"Jesus returned to Galilee in the power of the Spirit and news about Him spread through the whole countryside."

Most church members live so far below the standard, you'd have to backslide to be in fellowship. We are so subnormal that if we were to become normal, people would think we were abnormal![1]

—Vance Havner

Why Am I Not Experiencing the Holy Spirit's Power?

B ack in the 1930s Ira Yates owned a sheep ranch. Due to economic fallout from the Great Depression, he couldn't make ends meet and was forced to rely on government subsidy for years. Even with government support he couldn't make all the mortgage payments for his property. Just as Yates was on the verge of losing his farm, a seismographic crew drilled for oil on his property. Yates knew it was a long shot, but what did he have to lose?

To say they found oil is an understatement. The first well produced 80,000 barrels a day, which, by today's standards, is equivalent to millions of dollars' worth of oil every twenty-four hours. Thirty years later, analysis of the property revealed it still had the capacity to generate 125,000 barrels of oil a day.

Yates legally owned the oil the day he bought the ranch, yet for years he lived in virtual poverty. He wasn't aware of the wealth at his disposal and that lack of awareness diminished the quality of his life.[2]

Isn't the same true for many Christians? Don't some of us live in spiritual poverty because we're unaware of the divine resources available to us? Don't some of us eke out a bland existence rather than enjoy our God-given potential?

One author says, "When we look at God's marvelous provision for victorious living, and then consider the actual experience of Christians, we are astonished at the amazing gap between these two things."[3]

Andrew Murray assessed the quality of life experienced by most Christians he knew. He didn't see evidence of the Holy Spirit's power in their lives or their ministries. The following characteristics grieved him:

- Lack of power over patterns of sin among church members.

- Little distinction between them and the world.

- Lack of persistence with spiritual disciplines and growth in faith.

- Either lack of concern for, or ineffectiveness in reaching, the unconverted.

- Unwillingness to sacrifice in order to extend God's kingdom in the world.[4]

How would Murray rate the spiritual experience of the Christians you know? Would there be any difference? For some perhaps, but for the vast majority probably not much of one.

Is it any wonder that the small number who rely on the Holy Spirit's provision for victorious living are dubbed "super" Christians? Such folks aren't extraordinary, however. In fact the New Testament would label them "normal." According to A.W. Tozer,

> The Spirit indwelt life is not a special deluxe edition of Christianity to be enjoyed by a certain rare and privileged few who happen to be made of finer and more sensitive stuff than the rest. Rather, it is the normal state for every redeemed man and woman the world over.[5]

Billy Graham echoes Tozer's sentiments:

> The Spirit-filled life is not abnormal; it is the normal Christian life. Anything less is subnormal; it is less than what God wants and provides for His children. Therefore, to be filled with the Spirit should never be thought of as an unusual or unique experience for, or known by, only a select few.[6]

In Chapters 2 and 3 you examined the powerful effects the Holy Spirit has on a person who is yielded to Him. Perhaps that survey of His works whetted an appetite within you for a more *experiential* knowledge of His power. This chapter identifies causes and characteristics of spiritual poverty, describes a person who takes the Holy Spirit for granted and helps you discover a way to escape such an impoverished existence.

We don't know whether your heart is soft and tender or parched and dry, but we do know that God's Word can drill through the hardest heart. For the next few minutes, use His Word to tap into the bounty offered by the Holy Spirit. What you uncover won't change your net worth, *just your life*.

Ready to start drilling?

Causes of Spiritual Poverty

Why are "normal" Christians so few and far between? Why do so many who believe in Christ live below the spiritual poverty level? Three factors that contribute to spiritual poverty stand out.

1. *Lack of the Holy Spirit's presence in their lives.* Escaping spiritual poverty is impossible without the Holy Spirit's enabling power. Even so, many religious people do not have the Holy Spirit living in them. Romans 8:9 reads: "You are not in the flesh but in the Spirit, if indeed the Spirit of God dwells in you. *But if anyone does not have the Spirit of Christ, he does not belong to Him*" (emphasis added). Therefore people who lack the presence of the Holy Spirit in their lives are living in spiritual poverty because they are not really Christians at all. They may *profess* a relationship with Christ, yet they do not *possess* a relationship with Him. Perhaps they confuse a mental acknowledgment of truth ("I believe in God and the Bible") with saving faith. Yet just

nodding in agreement with Bible truths doesn't make anyone a Christian.

Q Consult Mark 1:23-24 and Mark 5:1-7. **What basic truth about Jesus did even demons acknowledge?**

A *Jesus was the Holy One of God. Jesus was the Son of the most High God*

Q Read James 2:19. **How does this verse show that "right doctrine" alone doesn't make a person a Christian?**

A *Even the demons believe & shudder at right doctrine.*

Entering a relationship with Jesus Christ involves a grace-motivated response of your will. He enters your life by a personal invitation which involves agreeing with Him that you've sinned and need a Savior. It means acknowledging His right to rule your life. It requires a change of mind about your lifestyle, being fed up with the status quo, willing to shuck behavior patterns that displease God.

No matter how religious a person is, without a genuine conversion experience he cannot develop Christlikeness or engage in fruitful ministry.

2. *Lack of instruction about the Holy Spirit's presence and/or potential.* Some folks who receive Christ as Savior haven't been taught about the

Holy Spirit. He indwells them, but His potential lies untapped because they don't realize His availability to help them.

Remember Ira Yates, the poor sheep rancher who eked out a living, unaware that his property held oil worth billions? Christians who remain ignorant of the Holy Spirit's presence within them are like that: teeming with wealth, but unaware of it. They've heard what Christ did for them on the cross, they know they have been forgiven the *penalty* of sin, but they haven't heard how the Holy Spirit provides the *power* to overcome sin.

Here's Billy Graham's assessment of this problem: "Many of the young people I meet are living defeated, disillusioned, and disappointed lives even after coming to Christ. They are walking after the flesh because they haven't had proper teaching at this precise point."[7]

Mull over Romans 8:10-13.

Q What miraculous historical act illustrates the power of the Holy Spirit who indwells you?

A *The resurrection of Jesus Christ*

Q What words/phrases from these verses reveal the impact or effects the Holy Spirit can have in your life?

A *your spirit is alive because of righteousness. no obligation to sin but put to death the misdeeds of the body.*

3. *Lack of obedience to God's will in Scripture.*
Many believers start out on the right foot. Their conversion experience was valid. For years, they successfully resist temptation and engage in fruitful ministry. But as they grow older they become spiritually complacent. Perhaps they take their growth for granted by withdrawing from faith-strengthening fellowship. Or they get sporadic in their intake of Scripture or become inconsistent in prayer. Then in a moment of vulnerability, they yield to sin. As a result of disobedience they lose spiritual power for a time because the Holy Spirit empowers only those who are fully yielded to Christ.

Jerry Bridges explains how our choices may drain our spiritual reservoir:

> It is time for us Christians to face up to our responsibility for holiness. Too often we say we are "defeated" by this or that sin. No, we are not defeated; we are simply disobedient! It might be well if we stopped using the terms "victory" and "defeat" to describe our progress. Rather we should use the terms "obedience" and "disobedience." When I say I am defeated by something, I am unconsciously slipping out from under my responsibility. I am saying something outside of me has defeated me. But when I say I am disobedi-

ent, that places the responsibility for my sin
squarely on me. We may, in fact, be defeated, but
the reason we are defeated is because we have
chosen to disobey. We have chosen to entertain
lustful thoughts, or to harbor resentment, or to
shade the truth a little.[8]

Now you know: Even someone who has lived
in dependence on the Holy Spirit can choose a
route that leads to spiritual poverty. *finish poorly*.

Q What reaction do you have to the possibility
of becoming a spiritual pauper? How can
awareness of this possibility affect you posi-
tively?

A *I do want to "finish well" Con-*
tinually hold onto God's Word,
prayer, church and suffering as
means of grace from God.

Now let's shift the spotlight to characteristics
of spiritual poverty.

Characteristics of Spiritual Poverty

Here's how one author describes a Christian
living in spiritual poverty: "He has a life of un-
ceasing conflict . . . repeated defeat . . . protracted
infancy . . . barren fruitlessness, adulterous infi-
delity, and dishonoring hypocrisy. Romans 7 is
his permanent address."[9]

What does it mean to reside in Romans 7? It is a
chapter describing the inner turmoil of a person
who is living in spiritual poverty. It is about the
experience of an individual who yearns to live

righteously, but feels pulled to evil like iron filings
to a magnet. Romans 7 is about the famous apos-
tle Paul's experience as he tried to live the Christian life under the law, relying on his own effort,
rather than the provision of the Holy Spirit.[10]

Q Read Romans 7:14-24 slowly. **What words/
phrases from the text reveal Paul's desire to
live a godly life?**

A *What I want to do, I do not do; I
have the desire to do what is good, but
I cannot carry it out. In my inner
being, I delight in God's law. Who will
rescue me?!*

Q Find words/phrases from this passage that
explain why Paul failed to do so.

A *Sin nature within. The evil I do
not want to do, I keep doing. Sin
living in me does it. Law of sin
waging war against the law of my mind.*
(making me a prisoner of the law of sin.)

Q What words most accurately describe the
emotional state, or attitude, of someone experiencing the dilemma of Romans 7:14-24?

A *Defeated, discouraged, frustrated
without joy, purpose or power
or peace*

This passage paints at least three characteristics
of someone living in spiritual poverty.

Frustrated. The Christian living in spiritual poverty is frustrated because, according to Romans
7:15, he is not practicing what he would like to do.
He tries to be a good husband and father, to obey

Christ's commands and to serve the church faithfully, but finds himself powerless. He doesn't have the spiritual energy necessary to do that which he knows he should do and, for that matter, wants to do. This lack of ability leads to extreme frustration.

Defeated. According to Romans 7:19 a spiritually impoverished Christian practices the very evil he does not wish to do—which is even worse than not doing what he wants to do. As a result, his love for others wanes and his passion for God grows cold. He neglects his prayer life and has no desire to spend time in the Word of God. A vibrant relationship with Christ is replaced by a legalistic routine. Impure thoughts, criticism and worry consume him. Sin defeats and discourages him.

Miserable. Not only is he frustrated because he *is not* doing what he does want to do, and defeated because he *is* doing what he does not want to do, but a Christian living in spiritual poverty is also miserable. Romans 7:24 says, "Wretched man that I am! Who will set me free from the body of this death?" Hearing someone talk about the abundant, dynamic, victorious Christian life makes him think, *You have got to be kidding. I'm trying to live a Christian life, but it just isn't working.*

Contemplate the causes and characteristics of spiritual poverty. The only way to ensure that the study of the causes and characteristics of spiritual poverty does not become merely a theoretical exercise is to connect it to your own life. Consider the following question.

Q To what extent do the characteristics of spiritual poverty describe *your* Christian life?

A *I am a frustrated, defeated, and miserable wife. Obsessing over my marital conditions keeps me from moving on with Christ.*

No doubt every believer experiences some degree of spiritual frustration and defeat. But the issue in Romans 7 is an ongoing pattern of defeat, not an occasional slip. If you or someone you love currently lives in the slums of Romans 7, chances are you're thinking about a relocation. What's involved in escaping such spiritual poverty?

Reserve your U-Haul, and proceed to the next section.

Conquering Spiritual Poverty

Paul identifies the fundamental means of escaping spiritual poverty in Galatians 5:16-18. Pore over those three verses for a few minutes.

Q What contrasts can you find in these verses?

A *Sinful nature vs. Spirit. Sinful nature doing what you do not want vs. living by Spirit, free from law of sin*

Q What phrases in 5:16 and 18 tell how to prevent spiritual bankruptcy?

A *Live by the Spirit, be led by the Spirit*

Paul's passage identifies two types of Christians:
those who walk according to the flesh and those
who "walk by the Spirit" (5:16). The Greek term
translated "flesh" refers to the innate bent toward
sin within every person. It's a reference to the moral
frailty of man *apart from supernatural assistance*.

A Christian who walks according to the flesh
seeks to live the Christian life in his or her own en-
ergies and efforts. This kind of Christian is like a
man who has been toiling along the road, bending
under a heavy burden. Soon a wagon overtakes him
and the driver kindly offers to help him on his journey. He joyfully accepts the offer but, when seated
in the wagon, continues to bend beneath the burden
he keeps on his shoulders. Concerned, the kind-
hearted driver asks, "Why do you not lay down
your burden?" "Oh!" replies the man, "I feel that it
is enough to ask you to carry me. I could not possibly ask you to carry my burden too." These Christians, having trusted Christ for their salvation, act as
though it is too much to trust Christ for the power
to live the Christian life here on earth. As a result
they bear their own burdens, and living the Christian life becomes drudgery.

The second type of Christian, however, is the
Christian that walks in the Spirit. That is, he al-
lows the Holy Spirit to live the Christian life
through him. He has reached a point where he
can bear the burden no more and longs to lay it on
the shoulders of Christ. As one author put it,

(1) With some there is a longing for peace and joy and unbroken fellowship with the Lord, a new life of loving the Word of God and drawing near to God in prayer. (2) With some it is longing to be delivered from some besetting sin and to have victory, especially in the little temptations that may mar the daily walk. (3) With others there is the longing that they might be soul-winners, that there might be greater power in their testimony to other lives and in the results obtained in ministering to others.[11]

Do you remember when you first became a Christian? Do you remember the peace and joy that filled your heart? Do you remember the confidence that you had then and how certain you were that the Lord who had saved you with His mighty power would surely give you victory in the months and years to come?

What has been your experience? Have you, like so many Christians, forgotten what it means to allow God's Spirit to live His life through you? Have you put the burden of life back on your own shoulders? Are you trying to pump the living waters of the Spirit rather than allowing them to pump you? Have you chosen to live in spiritual poverty rather than experiencing the victorious Christian life that is yours to enjoy? If so, you know deep in your heart that your experience is not all that God has for you.

You can escape the frustration of always trying to live the Christian life but finding it dry, boring and irrelevant. You can break the constant cycle

of telling God you will do better, yet finding yourself once again defeated by deeply ingrained sinful habits. You can find relief from the pattern of
sinning, repenting, begging forgiveness and telling God you will definitely do better next time,
only to fail again. You can escape the misery associated with spiritual poverty and tap into all the
joy of heaven.

The key? Instead of trying to live the Christian
life *for* Him, allow Him to live the Christian live
through you.

Q Why would a Christian *not* want to escape
spiritual poverty and appropriate the victorious Christian life that the Spirit provides?

A *Fear, lack of faith in God's
provision, perhaps ignorance, pride,
unwillingness to repent of disobedience.*

Q If you have been living in spiritual poverty,
do you want to escape? Why?

A *I did & I did. the burden
of "sweatsuit" Christianity robbed
me of joy and peace.*

How then does one walk in the Holy Spirit and
escape spiritual poverty? The following three commands give tremendous insight on how to do this.

- Ephesians 4:30: "Do not grieve the Holy
  Spirit of God."

- Ephesians 5:18: "Be filled with the Spirit."

- First Thessalonians 5:19: "Do not quench the Spirit."

In the next three chapters you will look at each of these commands so you may learn how to walk in the Spirit and live the Christian life the way God intended.

Memory Verse

Hide the following Bible verses in your heart this week: Galatians 5:19-21.

"The acts of the sinful nature are obvious; sexual immorality, impurity, and debauchery; idolatry and witchcraft; hatred, discord, jealousy, fits of rage, selfish ambition, dissensions, factions, and envy; drunkenness, orgies, and the like. I warn you, as I did before, that those who live like this will not inherit the kingdom of God."

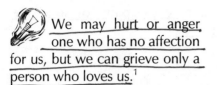
How Do I Grieve the Holy Spirit?

Sarah, in her early 80s, resides in a nursing home. Neither of her two grown children has visited, called or written in over six months. Both of them live within a 200-mile radius.

* * *

The most recent argument between Bob and his teenage son was the worst yet. The flare-up ended when his son gritted his teeth and spewed the words: *"I hate you!"*

* * *

Betty just received word that her eighteen-year-old daughter, a college freshman, had an abortion. She raised her daughter on Christian values and had every reason to believe her daughter's faith would sustain her when she was on her own.

What do Sarah, Bob and Betty have in common? *Grief.* The verb *grieve* is actually a love word. As the quotation at the start of this chapter points out, it means to cause pain for someone who cares deeply for us.

Grieving God

Scripture teaches that you can grieve the heart of God. More specifically, when you sin—when you choose to disregard His commands and plans for your life—you grieve the Holy Spirit. "Do not grieve the Holy Spirit of God, by whom you were sealed for the day of redemption" (Ephesians 4:30).

Chapter 4 of this book identified two types of Christians. Some believers walk according to the flesh by attempting to please the Lord through their own strength and energy. The result is spiritual poverty. Other believers rely daily on the Holy Spirit's power, tapping into divine resources for the capacity to live a distinctively Christian lifestyle.

This chapter focuses on how a Christian may grieve the Holy Spirit. It's impossible to experience His power and escape from spiritual poverty if our choices and conduct consistently grieve Him. Here's how Bill Bright puts it:

> Whenever we commit a sin—particularly if we continue to live in that sin, without confessing it before Him—the Holy Spirit . . . is grieved. He becomes saddened because we are not experiencing the joy of living supernaturally in close fellowship with Him.[2]

Picture the two valves of a water faucet—*hot* and *cold*. Each valve can be either on or off, so four options exist regarding the status of the faucet.

1. The hot valve is on while the cold valve is on.
2. The hot valve is on while the cold is off.
3. The hot valve is off while the cold is on.
4. The hot valve is off and the cold is off.

Let the hot valve represent "walking in the Spirit," and the cold valve represent "walking in the flesh." Regarding the status of your Christian life, option 1 is not a possibility. You cannot walk in the Spirit and walk in the flesh simultaneously. According to Galatians 5:17, "The flesh sets its desire against the Spirit, and the Spirit against the flesh; for these are in opposition to one another, so that you may not do the things that you please." Perhaps it is possible to "live in neutral"—to live with both valves off—when you aren't enslaved by either the Holy Spirit or fleshly desires. But it is impossible for both valves to be on at the same time.

In the terms of this analogy, when your "flesh valve" is on and the "Spirit valve" is off, grieving the Holy Spirit is inevitable.

In view of what you've learned so far, complete the following sentence in twenty-five words or less:

Q To grieve the Holy Spirit means

 you have rejected the Holy Spirit help in living the Christian life, and have decided to do it on your own and in your own way.

Ways We Grieve God

Since we grieve the Holy Spirit when we surrender to deeds of the flesh, let's examine Galatians 5:19-21. There you'll find a list of things that cause the Lord grief.

> Now the deeds of the flesh are evident, which are: immorality, impurity, sensuality, idolatry, sorcery, enmities, strife, jealousy, outbursts of anger, disputes, dissensions, factions, envying, drunkenness, carousing, and things like these. . . ."

Let's put each under our mental microscope separately:

- *Immorality* is a general word describing a compromise of God's standards. In this passage immorality refers specifically to the compromise of God's standards for sexual purity. The term encompasses outward behavior, such as extramarital sex, as well as inward impurity of the mind and heart. "The Greek word here is broad enough to cover all kinds of sexual wickedness and is, incidentally, the word *porneia*, from which the term *pornography* comes."[3]

- *Impurity* is a more narrow term than immorality, and it usually refers to the inner person: one's motives and thoughts. Imagine your throat aches from thirst and you're offered a cold glass of clear spring water. You'd gulp it down immediately.

But if you spotted a single drop of sewage in the glass of water, you'd hesitate to drink it no matter how thirsty you were. The water is too impure to entice you. Yet our impurity is much more revolting to a holy God than a drop of sewage in water is to us.

Thought life is a common spiritual battleground for many Christians. Satan works overtime to pollute our thoughts, knowing that wrong thinking results in wrong behavior and a stained character.

Q **What are some common threats to a pure thought life in our culture?**

A _Television, movies, newspapers, magazines, books, internet_

Q Read Proverbs 4:23. **What are some concrete ways to guard or watch over our hearts?**

A _Screen all the above through a biblical filter, and avoid impurity in any form_

- _Sensuality_ carries a different shade of meaning than either immorality or impurity. An immoral or impure person may try to hide his sexual sin from others. But what distinguishes a sensual person is the lack of embarrassment or apology concerning his behavior. Sensuality implies a flaunting of a lifestyle that's abhorrent to the Lord. "This

Say Paradise

deed of the flesh refers to one who has an
<u>insolent contempt for public opinion, and</u>
<u>shamefully outrages public decency.</u>"[4]

Q How is a sensual lifestyle the result of or the eventual outcome of impurity and immorality?

A *"Your mind will Take you thue!"*
"What is hidden will be revealed."

---

* *Idolatry* <u>occurs when people worship or</u>
  <u>value something or someone other than or</u>
  <u>more than God Himself.</u> In biblical times
  idols were usually handmade figurines carved
  from wood or stone. Pagan cultures have
  worshiped rocks, trees, animals—you name
  it. Few folks in modern societies bow down
  to literal idols but it is common to desire or
  value another person, a particular job, money
  or reputation more than God.

Q What things often compete with God for your allegiance?

A _____

Q Read Colossians 3:5. **What did Paul equate with idolatry?**

A *Sleep, my husband, learning*

- *Sorcery* is "the use of power gained from the assistance or control of evil spirits."[5] Synonymous with witchcraft, it comes from the Greek term *pharmakia*, from which we derive *pharmacy*. The word connotes the use of magical potions or drugs to invoke the aid of evil spirits. You grieve the Holy Spirit when you dabble in witchcraft, astrology, tarot cards, Ouija boards—anything having to do with supernatural forces other than the Person of God.

- *Enmities* is the first of several words dealing with relational problems. This term comprises anything from intense dislike to hatred. This negative attitude may express itself in verbal or physical abuse, and ranges from mere repugnance to open hostility.

- *Strife* refers to the result of bad attitudes—friction in human relationships. Too often it is a description of relationships among Christians.

Q Read Proverbs 17:14 and Philippians 2:3-4. What attitudes or behaviors can prevent strife?

A Curtail problem before it builds
Consider others and their best interest
before your own

- *Jealousy* shows in a possessiveness toward others whom we say we love. What matters in the relationship is whether our

needs or desires are being met. Jealousy
creates an atmosphere of suspicion and
distrust, often resulting in resentment.

Q In what sense is a jealous person a selfish person?

A They want the other person to
meet all their needs and desires
exclusively.

- *Outbursts of anger* occur when a person
feels insulted or belittled. This is a strong,
passionate emotion which can also be labeled rage or fury. (Irrational thinking
usually stems from the soil of uncon-
trolled anger, resulting in words and behavior that one later regrets.)

Q Read Proverbs 14:29, 17:27 and 25:28. **What
words and phrases from these verses represent
the opposite of "outbursts of anger"?**

A Understanding, restraint,
even-tempered, self-control

Q Mull over Proverbs 22:24-25. **Why are we
told to avoid hot-tempered people?**

A They may teach us our
ways; we may be ensared
by his/her actions.

- *Disputes* occur when a person feels he has to win an argument or prove a point. To wrangle with harsh words over who is right is a deed of the flesh. The word refers to self-seeking motives that spur divisive language between people.

Q According to Proverbs 15:1 what approach can relieve or minimize a dispute?

A *a gentle response as answer*

- *Dissension* is often the result of a dispute or disagreement. It's the ultimate division or ongoing discord that destroys relationships.
- *Factions* go a step further than dissension because groups of people are involved. Factions occur when two groups differ on a decision or issue, resulting in verbal jousts and divisiveness. The word connotes a selfish attitude on the part of people who fail to consider the good of the larger group or what course of action would bring glory to God.

Q What are the consequences of factions that develop in local churches?

A *Splits, disillusionment among seekers or new Christians, plant seeds of enmity, negative witness to unbelievers*

Q Look up First Corinthians 3:1-9. **How did Paul address factions in the church at Corinth?**

A *as spiritually emmature*

- *Envyings* refer to a resentful attitude one has toward someone else's good fortune. It is yet another form of selfishness that seeks the honor or possessions of others.

Q What most often engenders envy within your heart?

A *Romantic, intimate marriage relationships*

- *Drunkenness* is a result of imbibing too much alcohol. A drunken person loses control of speech, motor function and logical decision-making ability. It grieves the Holy Spirit because one temporarily yields control of his life to a foreign substance, usurping God's right to control him.

Q Digest the words of First Corinthians 6:19-20. **What reason does Paul give for maintaining control of your body?**

A *It belongs to God, is indwelt by Holy Spirit—purchased at a high price—the death of Christ.*

- *Carousings* are often associated with drunkenness. The word refers to group behavior that is immoral or out of control. In Paul's era, carousings referred to "a riotous procession of half-drunken and frolicsome fellows who, after supper, parade through the streets with torches and music in honor of Bacchus or some other false deity."[6] Though the purpose is fun, a more common consequence is regret.

Q Why does an individual often display less self-restraint in a group setting?

A *Peer pressure, wants to feel part of group, approval among his friends, sense of belonging—*

The "deeds of the flesh" in Galatians 5:19-21 are representative rather than exhaustive. Other ways we grieve Him are hinted at in descriptions of the Holy Spirit. For instance, He is in the Spirit of:

- *Truth* (John 14:17). Anything that is deceitful or hypocritical causes Him grief.

- *Holiness* (Romans 1:4). Whatever defiles a person's character or makes him worldly grieves Him.

- *Grace* (Hebrews 10:29). When we take the blood Jesus shed on the cross for granted or treat it flippantly, He is grieved.

Q What other examples of fleshly deeds can you think of that would grieve the Spirit?

A *lack of faith, worry, self-absorption, denial, running away from truth*

What happens to you when you grieve the Holy Spirit? Billy Graham says,

> When I commit one sin, one disobedient act, one departure from the clearly seen pathway of the will and the fear of God, then the ministry of the Spirit in my life is impaired. . . . To grieve the Holy Spirit is not to lose Him in my life. . . . But when He is grieved, He does bring about an absence of joy and power in our lives until we renounce and confess the sin. Though we may appear happy, we are inwardly wretched.[7]

The next section examines deterrents to grieving the Spirit.

Deterrents to Grieving the Spirit

To avoid grieving the Spirit, you must first realize you don't have to give in to the desire of the flesh, which ultimately leads to the deeds of the flesh mentioned above. Let us repeat. You do *not* have to give in. Sound unbelievable? Not according to Romans 6:6-7 which says, "Knowing this, that our old self was crucified with Him, in order that our body of sin might be done away with, so that we would no longer be slaves to sin; for he who has died is freed from sin." According to these verses, before you became a Christian you were a slave to your sinful tendencies, but the moment you became a Christian you were freed from the power of the flesh. The phrase "done away with" in the original language means to "render idle."[8] So the desire of the flesh, though still present in your life, has been made powerless. It may still seek to exert its influence but you are no longer under its power. You are free to say "no" to sin.

Q Do you really think *you* can say "no" to the influence of the flesh? Why or why not?

A *Yes but I must turn, take some action, way of escape from temptation trusting God to help you carry through*

Though you are free of its power, from time to time you may find yourself giving in to the relentless temptations of the flesh. If so, confess your sin immediately. First John 1:9 says, "If we confess our sins, He is faithful and righteous to forgive us our sins and to cleanse us from all unrighteousness." To confess means to agree with God that what you did was wrong.

Q Why do you think these are the first steps to leaving spiritual poverty and enjoying the dynamic Christian life?

A *Fellowship with God is only possible when sin is covered through blood of Christ and confession*

Are you grieving the Holy Spirit by saying "yes" to the ungodly influence of the flesh? If you are, you will continue living in spiritual poverty. You will never experience the dynamic Christian life that is yours to possess.

Memorizing Scripture and Application

Plant the words of Ephesians 4:30 deeply into the soil of your heart. They are a reminder that <u>God loves you so much that it is possible to hurt Him with your behavior.</u>

Also, read Ephesians 4:29. A study of the Greek language reveals a direct grammatical link between verses 29 and 30 in Ephesians 4. What Paul said about grieving the Holy Spirit stems directly from the command in 4:29.

Q Based on Ephesians 4:29, describe one additional way Christians may grieve the Holy Spirit.

A *Unwholesome talk, talk that does not help build up others according to their needs, for their benefit*

Q In what way are you most prone to grieve Him with words?

A *Talking about Bob negatively.*

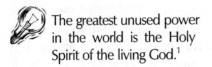

How Do I Quench the Holy Spirit?

Chances are you associate the word "quench" with TV commercials. You see a sweat-soaked tennis player gulping some new sports drink or a beaming member of Generation X soothing his parched throat with a popular soda. They're pushing a particular drink as a way to quench your thirst. This use of "quench" puts a positive spin on the term. It's synonymous with words like "satisfy" or "fulfill." But in this chapter the word takes a different slant.

Defining "Quench"

When we refer to *quenching* the Holy Spirit, the word carries a negative connotation. To "quench" the Holy Spirit means "to extinguish" or "to put out a fire."[2] You quench the Holy Spirit when you nullify or restrict His power. Just as you toss water on a campfire to quench the flames, you can douse the fire of God's Spirit through particular attitudes and behaviors. Bill Bright wrote, "We are not to live in sin or to allow sin to go unconfessed in our lives. If we do, then we put out the Holy Spirit's fire in our lives."[3]

Another way to grasp the concept of quenching the Spirit is to employ the faucet analogy from the previous chapter in this book. Turning on the hot water valve is tantamount to allowing God's Spirit to have His own way. Turning on the cold water valve is analogous to allowing the sinful nature (the flesh) to dominate. As explained in Chapter 5, *grieving* the Holy Spirit occurs when you turn on fleshly desires. But *quenching* the Holy Spirit occurs when you merely turn off His desires or resources. Whereas grieving God's Spirit involves wrongdoing, quenching the Spirit may not involve commission of outright sin. You quench Him by failure to tap into His power for good by resisting what He wants to do for you, in you and through you. Put simply, grieving Him is saying "yes" to the flesh. Quenching Him is saying "no" to God.

Condense what you've read so far by completing the following sentence in twenty words or less:

Q To "quench the Holy Spirit" means

A *is to reject what God wants to do for you, in you, and through you.*

Demonstrating a Quenching of the Holy Spirit

To discuss *how* a Christian can quench the Holy Spirit, we'll employ the following organizational framework. You can refuse what the Holy Spirit wants to do *for you*, reject what He wants to do *in you* and resist what He wants to do *through you.*

Refusing His Work *for You*

One thing the Holy Spirit wants to do for you is to provide insight and understanding. To put it another way, *He wants to impress on your heart and mind biblical perspectives that reassure you.* According to First Corinthians 2:12, "Now we have received, not the spirit of the world, but the Spirit who is from God, *so that we may know the things freely given to us by God*" (emphasis added).

The Holy Spirit accomplished this for Bill years ago as he was stretched out on the floor spending his "quiet time" with the Lord. (His physical posture didn't reflect extraordinary spirituality on his part. It was his way of edging closer to the only heater in his house!) God's Spirit impressed upon his mind the implications of Christ's death on the cross for him. As he meditated on Scripture, his value to the Lord became clearer. He grasped with his affections, not just with his head, that God's acceptance of him is based on Christ's perfection and work—not on his own performance. A simple yet profound truth concerning his identity in Christ took root in the soil of his heart that day. If he had refused to believe the implications of the cross, he would have quenched the Holy Spirit's work. What He did for Bill was to reassure him of God's unconditional love.

Another way in which the Spirit wants to work for us relates to our experience of stress or suffering. *He yearns to comfort us during times of special need.* That's why Jesus used the term "Helper" or "Comforter" (LB) to describe the Holy Spirit (John 14:16). The road to heaven is dotted with potholes. Rather than shielding us from adversity, God offers His presence and supernatural peace during difficulties. When we're hurting, we refuse the Holy Spirit's comfort by complaining or by distancing ourselves from means of grace such as prayer, Bible study and burden-bearing fellowship with other believers.

The Holy Spirit also wants to instill within you wisdom and guidance. Need to know how to handle a rebellious teenager? How to support a husband through a gut-wrenching midlife crisis? Whether to accept a new job opportunity that dropped in your lap? Then you want to experience what Paul called "being led by the Spirit of God" (Romans 8:14).

Though it isn't a conscious choice, Christians refuse the Holy Spirit's offer of wisdom and guidance when they avoid the means through which He provides for them: Bible study, prayer and the insights of other believers. Avoidance may not be intentional. Perhaps a person pushes down harder on the career accelerator and fails to expose himself to the church's teaching ministry. Or perhaps he is too undisciplined to digest God's Word on a daily basis. Or he would rather stay home and watch a movie on TV than join a small group where authentic fellowship occurs. We refuse what God wants to do for us when we neglect the ways in which He has chosen to meet us and empower us.

What the Holy Spirit wants to do for us includes ① provision of insight and understanding, ② comfort during hard times, plus ③ wisdom and guidance.

Q To what extent have you forfeited these benefits because of neglect or disobedience? Can you think of times in your life when you unintentionally quenched the Holy Spirit's work in one of these areas? Describe those times below:

A • Insight and understanding *when I refused Bob's support during my gallbladder surgery*

A • Comfort during hard times *when I drove myself in work to avoid my problems with Bob*

A • Wisdom and guidance *when I let my fear of losing Bob interfere with considering his needs over mine*

Rejecting His Work *in You*

The Holy Spirit yearns to cultivate the characteristics of Christ within you. He wants to change you from the inside out, to overhaul the attitudes and motives that spawn behavior. Here's how Paul put it in a letter to the Philippians: "It is God who is at work *in you*, both to will and to work for His good pleasure" (Philippians 2:13, emphasis added). Earlier in the same letter, Paul used Jesus as an example of the humility and selflessness needed for unity in a church: "Have this attitude *in yourselves* which was also in Christ Jesus" (2:5, emphasis added).

Imagine you start your day by oversleeping. You leap out of bed to wake the kids, knowing they're already late for school. But you find them parked in front of the TV, mesmerized by a cartoon channel. That's when you blow a gasket! You scream at the kids. You stomp into the kitchen to rustle up some food, slamming cereal bowls on the counter to show how upset you are. A few minutes later you rush back to your bedroom to dress, only to remember that the shoes you need are on the porch, splashed with mud from the day before. When you finally drop the kids off at school, you pull back onto the main highway only to discover bumper-to-bumper traffic. You proceed at a snail's pace because of a stalled car a mile up the road. As you sit behind the wheel, you're seething with anger and frustration. At that moment, the Holy Spirit pricks your conscience and rebukes your attitude. He reminds you to put the faulty alarm clock and traffic delay in proper perspective.

How do you respond? Do you reject His effort to remodel your attitude, then throw yourself a pity party? Or do you confess your impatience and ask the Lord to renew a right spirit within you?

What are some other "inside jobs" that the Holy Spirit wants to perform? He wants to purify the motives behind decisions you make; to nudge you to seek fellowship with God through prayer, Bible reading or songs of praise; to encourage you to resist a particular temptation or improper use of your time; to put the spotlight on a particular attitude that needs changing, or a personal trait that needs cultivating in your character; to convict you of an unforgiving spirit toward a person who has hurt you.

The inner workings of God's Spirit cited above are exemplary rather than exhaustive, but you may find them helpful as you think through times when you have rejected what He wanted to do within you in specific areas.

Put a check mark by two of the following ways the Spirit may work in you, and then describe a time when you intentionally or unintentionally rejected His desire to work in you in that fashion.

✓ identified an attitude or trait to change or cultivate

✓ nudged me to spend time in prayer

___ nudged me to read the Bible

___ nudged me to spend time praising Him through song

___ reminded me of His willingness to help against temptation

___ other (you fill in) _____

_____

a. Incident #1 *Recognized deepening resentment, bitter spirit toward critical neglectful behavior of my husband. I wanted to feel sorry for self, have sympathy of others, have them side with me. Instead of cultivating a forgiving spirit, I chose to be angry or a martyr.*

b.   Incident #2 *Instead of developing a regular discipline for prayer, I continue to pray "hit and miss"—not spending enough time in prayer to "listen" or pray for others needs.*

Resisting His Work *through* You

One author discusses the issue of Christians resisting the Holy Spirit's work through them in this way:

> It is one thing to work for God; it is another to have God work through us. We are often eager for the former. God is always desirous of doing the latter . . . the God who is the ruler of the universe does not want us to plan, worry, and work for Him. What he wants is not our plans, but our lives, that He may work HIS plans through us.[4]

The ultimate purpose of God working *for you* and *in you* is so that He can work *through you*. He wants to use you as a servant through whom He can minister to other believers and to a needy world. That's what Paul had in mind in Second Corinthians 5:19-20: "He has committed to us the word of reconciliation. Therefore, we are ambassadors for Christ." And in Acts 1:8 Luke echoed the fact that God wants to work through us to spread the gospel: "You will receive power when the Holy Spirit has come upon you; and you shall be My witnesses both in Jerusalem, and in all Judea and Samaria, and even to the remotest part of the earth."

In what ways do we tend to resist what the Holy Spirit yearns to do through us? When we continually turn down opportunities for lay ministry in our local church; when we yield to feelings of inadequacy when we're asked to take the reins of leadership in a service project; when we muzzle the voice of the Spirit urging us to share Christ with a coworker.

Q Describe a time when you believe you resisted the wooing of the Holy Spirit to serve other believers in your church.

A *Nursery when my children were young. Committees*

Q Describe an incident when you said "no" to the Spirit's desire for you to share your faith in Christ.

A *Street and door to door evangelism, "dropping in" EE evangelism*

So far we've defined the concept of "quenching" the Holy Spirit and discussed ways in which we quench Him. Now let's shift the spotlight to a more practical issue: *How can we keep from quenching the Spirit?*

Deterrents to Quenching the Spirit

If a forest fire has a stiff breeze at its back, the flames can spread faster than a man can run. A *Newsweek* story about a particular blaze told how the flames jumped a ravine, then scurried up a slope. It had been moving one tree at a time, but with a shift in the wind, flames engulfed huge areas of forest simultaneously. Whole acres were destroyed in a flash, in a phenomenon firefighters call a "blow up."[5]

Two elements are needed for an outdoor fire to burn: *fuel* (brush or trees) and *oxygen* (wind). This is analogous to the Holy Spirit: for His flame to blaze in and through your life, you must give Him fuel and oxygen. The paragraphs that follow describe what constitutes "fuel" and "oxygen" in the spiritual realm.

The Holy Spirit's primary fuel supply is the Bible. According to Billy Graham, "A fire goes out when the fuel supply is withdrawn. When we do not stir up our souls, when we do not use means of grace . . . or read the Word of God, the fire of the Holy Spirit is banked."[6] Graham's words echo the sentiments of George Mueller: "The vigor of our spiritual life will be in exact proportion to the place held by the Bible in our life and thoughts."[7] Scripture is the means through which the Holy Spirit encourages, convicts and guides, so your sensitivity to God's Spirit will be in direct proportion to your exposure to God's Word. You are less likely to quench Him when you digest the words He has inspired.

Q In what specific ways are you exposing yourself to Scripture? (Include group studies you attend as well as personal, private study.)

A *Bible Certificate work, BSF, Bible-praying devotional books on praise and intercession*

Q What Bible learning opportunities do you need to take more advantage of?

A *just personal reading*

The way to increase the flow of oxygen and fan the flames of the Holy Spirit is by *cultivating an openness to, or awareness of, His inner promptings.* God may "speak" to you by means of subjective impressions or a "still small voice." Charles Swindoll uses the doctrine of creation—God's image within man—to explain how God is able to communicate with humans in ways distinct from other creatures.

> An entire system of communication is established at the time of salvation, making it possible to receive whatever it is the Holy Spirit wishes to communicate. . . . Such an inner system provides for the reception of divine information and the understanding of biblical truths, unknown to the animal kingdom. . . . That explains why we can hear His "still small voice" and decipher messages of peace or warning, conviction or guidance.[8]

Don't equate "inner promptings" or "subjective impressions" with new revelation from God. Though Swindoll acknowledges the "still small voice" of God's Spirit, he insists that *what the Spirit impresses upon us subjectively flows from what He has already revealed objectively*:

> Count on it—if it isn't between Genesis and Revelation, it is not divinely inspired, supernat-

urally infallible, or absolutely inerrant. You and
I don't need more revelation from God; what
we need is to observe and obey what He has already revealed in His book. If they are of the
Lord, those unidentified inner promptings
won't contradict anything biblically. The Lord
doesn't lead against His own revealed Word.[9]

John Piper salutes Swindoll's commentary and
adds the following perspective:

The claim to have an impression from the Lord
would need to conform to the teaching of Scripture, either to specific texts if any is immediately
relevant, or to the tenor, spirit, and trajectory of
the whole.[10]

What the Spirit conveys through inner promptings
may include clarification of a Bible truth, a fresh
awareness of a doctrine's practical implications for behavior or decision-making guidance influenced by an
eternal perspective or some biblical value. The fact
that God's Spirit communicates with us through inner
promptings is an example of divine truth that we can't
nail down and dissect with precision. However, we
also cannot deny it.

Speaking of this, Andrew Murray writes, "In
what does this leading consist? Chiefly in this, that
our whole hidden life is guided by Him to what it
ought to be." Murray goes on to say that

there are several different aspects of this leading.
When we read the Word, He leads us into a life
corresponding to the Word. When we pray He
leads us into the way in which to pray. As we

<u>grow in Christ-likeness, He leads us into all the will of God. When we speak and work, He leads us in power.</u>[11]

In this book we describe the leadership of the Holy Spirit as an inner prompting. This means the Holy Spirit is getting your attention in order to do something to you, in you or through you. To gain a better understanding of this, look at the chart below at some of <u>the characteristics of the Holy Spirit's promptings</u>.

Characteristics of the Holy Spirit's Promptings

THEY WILL *ALWAYS*	THEY WILL *NEVER*
• confirm Scripture	• contradict Scripture
• be specific	• be general
• convict	• condemn
• lead you	• push or drive you
• be simple	• be complicated
• motivate you to faith	• create fear in you
• focus primarily on changing you inwardly	• focus primarily on changing you outwardly
• emphasize character	• emphasize circumstances
• be true	• be false
• be clear	• be confusing
• restore relationships	• destroy relationships
• major on your faults, others' needs	• major on others' faults, your needs
• lead you to *do* something	• lead you to *overdo* something[12]

Q Describe a time when you were convinced that you received an inner prompting of the Holy Spirit.

A *Ask about observing at the Vineyard's Life Enrichment Center*

Q What convinces you that this inward impression came from the Holy Spirit? (Explain how the "message" you received confirmed, clarified or applied truth or values from Scripture.)

A *I had prayed the night before about whether I should commit to a ministry at Vineyard, and what He wanted me to do with my ESL training. The director mentioned the loss of the ESL teacher & desire to expand.*

How does one keep from quenching the Holy Spirit? You must give Him plenty of fuel by feeding often from the pages of Scriptures and plenty of oxygen by staying open to His promptings.

From the last two chapters you have learned that to walk in the Holy Spirit you must:

- confess any sin in your life,

- resist any and all temptation to give into the desires of the flesh,

- fuel the Spirit's fire by spending time in the Scriptures and

- feed the Spirit's fire by listening carefully in obedience to the Spirit's promptings.

Memorizing Scripture

Digest First Thessalonians 5:19 and be ready to recite the verse the next time your group meets.

"Do not put out the Spirits fire."

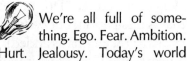 We're all full of something. Ego. Fear. Ambition. Hurt. Jealousy. Today's world needs people who are full of the Holy Spirit: men and women who are captivated, motivated and activated by the Spirit.[1]
—Stuart Briscoe

What Does It Mean to Be "Filled with the Holy Spirit"?

B ecause the Holy Spirit resides in every Christian, every believer has access to His power and divine enablement. This truth implies that no single person has a monopoly on the Holy Spirit. You will discover in this chapter, however, that *it is possible for the Holy Spirit to have a monopoly in an individual's life.*

Previous lessons introduced you to the Person of the Holy Spirit and surveyed His past and present works on your behalf. You discovered that He provides Christians with power to live extraordinary lives, but that many will live in spiritual poverty because they do not heed His inner promptings. We also pointed out that to understand how to escape this unfortunate state, you must examine what it means to grieve and quench the Holy Spirit.

Now the focus shifts to a controversial yet foundational concept: the filling of the Holy Spirit.

What did Paul mean when he wrote, "Do no get drunk with wine, for that is dissipation, but *be filled with the Spirit*"? (Ephesians 5:18, emphasis added).

Take this lesson to heart, and God's Spirit will have a monopoly on you.

What Is the Holy Spirit's "Filling"?

Grieving the Holy Spirit is a *love* word. Therefore, due to His deep love for you, your thoughts and behavior have the capacity to hurt God. *Quenching* the Spirit is a *fire* word that means to put out or to put a damper on. In reference to being filled with the Holy Spirit, *filling* is a *control* word.

In Ephesians 5:18, Paul contrasted a person filled wine with someone who is filled with the Holy Spirit. A drunken person yields control of his mind, tongue and body to alcohol. A person filled with God's Spirit yields control of his life to Him. Alcohol changes one's personality and behavior negatively, but the Holy Spirit puts a positive spin on character transformation.

Concentrate once again on the "faucet" analogy employed in previous chapters. One alternative is to turn off the Spirit valve and turn on the flesh valve. When that happens we grieve Him. When both valves are off, you're quenching the Spirit. Perhaps you aren't turning the "flesh" valve on, but you're resisting the means through which the Holy Spirit wants to work in your life. Another scenario in this analogy is for both the "hot" and "cold" water valves to be on simultaneously, but in the spiritual realm, that's impossible. The Spirit and the flesh "are in opposition to one another" (Galatians 5:17), so both forces can't be released in your life at the same time. A fourth possibility is to keep the flesh valve off while you turn on the Spirit valve. That's a state called the filling of the Holy Spirit.

Before proceeding with this lesson, let's clarify what we do *not* mean by the Holy Spirit's filling. *It does* not *mean to receive more of Him*. The moment you received Jesus Christ as Savior, the Holy Spirit took up residence in you. You can't get more of Him, because He's already present within you. Roy Hession emphasizes that "to be filled with the Holy Spirit is to be filled with one who is already there in our hearts."[2]

Though you can't get more of the Holy Spirit, *He can get more of you!* Keep in mind that the issue of "filling" deals not with the amount of the Spirit we possess, but with the amount of our lives that He possesses. The following household analogy may add clarity to the concept:

> So just as it is one thing to have a guest in your house living in some remote corner of the house where you scarcely know that he is there, and quite another thing to have the guest taking entire possession of the house, just so it is one thing to have the Holy Spirit dwelling way back in some hidden sanctuary of our being, and quite another thing to have the Holy Spirit taking entire possession of the house. In other words, it is one thing to have the Holy Spirit

merely dwelling in us but we are not conscious of His dwelling, and quite another thing to be filled . . . with the Holy Spirit.[3]

If *grieving* the Spirit is saying "yes" to the flesh and if *quenching* the Spirit is saying "no" to God, then being *filled* with the Spirit is saying "yes" to God and "no" to sin.

Q Using the previous paragraphs as food for thought, use your own words to write a one-sentence definition of "being filled with the Holy Spirit."

A *Giving control of your life to the Holy Spirit*

Now let's turn our attention to another question that should be percolating in our minds. *How can you tell when a person is filled with the Holy Spirit?*

How Does the Holy Spirit's "Filling" Show?

By examining the context of Paul's command to "be filled with the Spirit," along with several other Bible verses, you can identify ways in which the Holy Spirit's control manifests itself. Saturate yourself with the content of the following references.

Q Beside each Scripture reference, jot down one or more demonstrations of the Holy Spirit's control. Think about what is implied by the words you read, not just what is directly stated.

A 1. Acts 1:8: _power to witness_

_____

_____

A 2. First Corinthians 12:7-11: _use gifts to show God's love to others; loving, hate evil, honoring, spiritually enthusiastic, consistent, servant_

A 3. Galatians 5:19-25: _avoid acts of sinful nature (flesh) demonstrate love, joy, peace, patience, kindness, goodness, faithfulness, gentleness, self-control_

A 4. Ephesians 5:18-21: _Practice praise worship, thanksgiving with others & when alone; submit to others_

A 5. Second Peter 1:19-21: _Concentrate on God's Word as source of direction, inwardly & outwardly_

[margin note: filled w/ the Spirit]

A magazine article called "The Second Wind" says, "If an Olympian experiences a second wind, that is probably a sign that he is not in great shape. Scientists are divided over whether a second wind is purely psychological, the athlete willing himself forward. But if it has a physical basis, that sudden feeling of 'I can do it' right after 'I want to die' probably reflects a change in metabolism."[4]

Being filled with the Spirit is like a second wind. If you think, "I just can't live the Christian life. I want to quit. I am frustrated and discouraged," then you need a change in metabolism. When the Holy Spirit fills you, you suddenly go from "I can't go on" to "I can do all things through Him who strengthens me" (Philippians 4:13).

Philippians 2:13 says, "For it is God who is at work in you, both to will and to work for His good pleasure." According to this verse, the desire and power to live the Christian life comes from God Himself who indwells you. It is the Holy Spirit who enables you to do the good works for which you were created. This change in metabolism expresses itself in at least seven major ways, The Holy Spirit will give you the desire and power to have:

- *A heartfelt capacity to worship*. Worship is implied by Paul's reference to "speaking to one another in psalms and hymns and spiritual songs, singing and making melody with your heart to the Lord" (Ephesians 5:19). Worship is our response to God's revelation of Himself. A Spirit-filled person is more sensitive to who God is (His attributes) and what He has done. Whether the setting is a corporate church service or the recliner where you spend your daily quiet time seeking God, the Spirit will turn your thoughts toward God and instill a desire to praise Him.

Q Describe the most meaningful worship experience you've ever had as a Christian. Be sure to emphasize its Godward focus. What divine traits or deeds evoked your worship?

A *When I was alone—separated and rejected, at the Vineyard during praise time. I knew I would never be abandoned—God's love relationship with me is eternal*

- *A grateful attitude.* His filling results in our "giving thanks for all things in the name of our Lord Jesus Christ to God" (Ephesians 5:20). When He controls us, we don't take for granted His past work nor His present interventions on our behalf. Here's how Charles Swindoll puts it: "Show me a grumbler, and I'll show you a person who has distanced herself or himself from the Spirit of God. When we are filled with the Spirit . . . we are not hard to please . . . we are not spoiled or choosy."[5]

Q When you contemplate completing the following sentence, jot down the first three things that come to mind:

A   God, I want to thank You for . . .

1. *salvation in Christ*
2. *your gracious provisions*
3. *Your Word*

- *Authentic fellowship with other believers.*
  There's also a horizontal dimension to Ephesians 5:18-21. Spirit-filled believers speak
  and sing "to one another" (5:19). They are
  "subject to one another" rather than clamor-
  ing for rights or special privileges (5:21). In
  reference to the horizontal evidence of the
  Spirit's control, Swindoll adds,

> We want to hear what others have to
> say. We want to learn from one another.
> And we also want to contribute to each
> other's welfare. If we see our brothers
> and sisters in a dangerous or perilous sit-
> uation, we want to warn them.[6]

Q Describe one or two fresh expressions of fellowship that you've encountered over the past
year.

A *Meeting new Christians in new church
setting. corporate worship and
small groups; prayer, cards from
old Christian friends in can-ab treatment*

- *A new capacity and desire to overcome sinful
  habits.* If you refer back to Galatians 5:19-21,
  you will remember the deeds of the flesh. But
  5:22-23 goes on to add, "But the fruit of the
  Spirit is love, joy, peace, patience, kindness,
  goodness, faithfulness, gentleness, self-control;
  against such things there is no law." The bottom line truth from these verses is the need to
  rely on the Holy Spirit's power for holy living. You cannot overcome sin in your own

efforts; you must be filled with the Spirit. It is like flying in a plane. When you go through turbulent conditions the pilot often says, "We're going to give it a little more power to rise above the bad weather." Daily dependence on Him enables you to shed sinful patterns by flying above the storms of sinful habits. As you tap into His power daily, the fruit of Christlikeness becomes increasingly evident.

Q A habit or sinful pattern that the Holy Spirit has enabled me to overcome is

A *Compulsive eating for comfort or stress relief; insisting that Bob agree with me — I am still struggling with so many —!*

- A *greater desire and power for service.* In First Corinthians 12 Paul described another effect of the Spirit's filling: successful ministry through the exercise of spiritual gifts. When He controls you, the giftedness bestowed on you at salvation is released and its impact is magnified. You become willing to sacrifice in order to engage in kingdom business. (Chapter 11 delves into the topic of spiritual gifts in more detail.)

Q Think back over the past year. List specific ministries you've exercised (both formal and informal, public as well as behind-the-scenes). Also tell what spiritual gifts from the list in

First Corinthians 12:7-11 you believe you exercised in those contexts.

A *wisdom shared with Paula, Monica, Children; faith without signs of change in my marriage to keep hoping + trusting God sharing scriptural teaching & application.*

- *A greater appetite for and understanding of God's Word.* Since the Holy Spirit authored the Bible (2 Peter 1:19-21), it's only natural for a yielded person to digest His words. His control also enhances your understanding of Scripture since He crystallizes meaning for the honest seeker.

  The thoughts of God no one knows except the Spirit of God. Now we have received . . . the Spirit who is from God, so that we may know the things freely given to us by God. . . . But a natural man does not accept the things of the Spirit of God, for they are foolishness to him, and he cannot understand them, because they are spiritually appraised. (1 Corinthians 2:11-12, 14)

Q Since your conversion to Christ, how has your attitude toward and practice of Bible study changed?

A *It was through reading God's Word, I came to know Him. I have only grown to love it more through the years as I have tried to apply it to my life.*

- *A zeal for sharing your faith.* According to Acts 1:8 a consequence of the Holy Spirit's filling is power in witnessing. There are many ways to witness for Christ. You may not witness for Christ like Billy Graham, but when you are filled with the Spirit it does become easier for you to talk about Christ, because He's the most important Person in your life.

Q Since your conversion, to what extent has your attitude toward and practice of personal evangelism changed?

A *I see it as a focus of a Christian's life. I do speak to people about Christ — have trained with EE and navigators, I have*

Circle the words below that describe how you currently feel about sharing your faith. Be honest.

confused   reluctant   scared
excited   guilt-ridden   teachable

The above seven demonstrations of the Spirit's filling are the main characteristics that separate average Christians from normal Christians. The normal Christian life manifests the fruit, gifts and power of the Holy Spirit. The average Christian lives in spiritual poverty, so there is as much of a difference between an average Christian and a Spirit-filled Christian as there is between a Christian and a non-Christian. Someone said, "Being saved will bring you to heaven, but being Spirit-filled will

difficulty sharing, witness, teaching/preaching in text or personal relationships.

bring heaven to you."[7] Why? Because all of the resources of heaven are now at your disposal.

Personal Reflection

Q In view of the characteristics examined in
this chapter, who comes to mind when you
think of a Spirit-filled Christian? Why?

A *Jennifred Casement – She
displays the fruit of spirit,
serves with "words of wisdom" as
counsellor, teacher, mother friend.*

Q Which manifestation of a Spirit-filled life that
we've covered is most real in your own experience? Explain.

A *Exhortation and teaching which
the Holy Spirit displayed through me
in various ministries. Joy in pain
and suffering.*

Q Which evidence of the Spirit's control is most
lacking in your current experience? Explain.

A *Patience – I want my husband
to become my husband again –
now!*

Q At this time, do you consider yourself a
Spirit-filled person? Why or why not?

A *Yes. I have asked for the
filling, experienced it, but I
know that I have much more
to learn and experience of God's grace*

So far you have determined what it means to be
filled with the Holy Spirit and identified evi-

dences of His control over a Christian's life. You have evaluated your own life in light of these evidences. The next logical question concerns *how* to live under His control—especially if you don't perceive yourself as a Spirit-filled person. Before we broach the issue of how to be filled with the Spirit, let's employ an automobile analogy. The Holy Spirit's role within a believer is similar to the role of fuel in a car's fuel tank. When we try to run our lives apart from Him, it is like trying to move a car with an empty gas tank—we don't get very far. Actually though, all the fuel we need— the Holy Spirit—is readily available to us. Charles Swindoll explains it best:

> We as believers have all the fuel that is needed for all the power, insight, comfort, guidance, courage, and dynamic we will ever need. The question is, *how do we get the fuel flowing so we can operate our lives as God intended?*[8]

Memorizing Scripture

By memorizing Ephesians 5:18, you'll cultivate a keen awareness that the Spirit's filling is a command, not an optional extra, for Christians.

"Do not get drunk on wine, which leads to debauchery. Instead, be filled with the spirit."

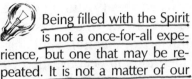
Being filled with the Spirit is not a once-for-all experience, but one that may be repeated. It is not a matter of our receiving more of Him. Rather it is a matter of relationship.[1]

CHAPTER EIGHT

How Can I Be Filled with the Holy Spirit?

When Bill was in sixth grade he was chosen to run the projector for a class showing of an educational film. This important responsibility allowed him to leave class, go down to the media center, get the projector and bring it back to his room. When he returned, he tried to plug the cord into the electric socket but could not because the prongs had been pulled apart. Being the creative type, he took his fingers and squeezed the prongs. Unfortunately they would not stay straight without being held. Not thinking, he held the prongs together so he could plug them into the electrical socket. When they connected with the power source Bill did a jig. He jumped up and down, his arm feeling like someone was pounding it with a hammer. He was plugged into a power source. Could he see the power? No. Was it evident in his life? Yes. His hair was sticking straight up.

In Chapter 7 you learned that the filling of the Holy Spirit is a matter of control. In contrast to a person under the influence of alcohol, Paul suggested that a Spirit-filled person is controlled by God: "And do not get drunk with wine, for that is dissipation, but be filled with the Spirit" (Ephesians 5:18). You determined what it means to be filled with the Holy Spirit and identified evidences of the Spirit's control over a Christian's life. Then you evaluated your own spiritual state in light of those evidences. Now the focus shifts to a more functional topic: _How can you experience the filling of the Holy Spirit? What perspectives and practices are needed to put a person under the control of the Holy Spirit?_

What follow are insights and strategies for experiencing the fullness of the Holy Spirit. Take the pointers in this lesson to heart, and you'll get plugged in to the ultimate power source . . . without the pain Bill experienced.

God's Part . . . and Yours

Examine Ephesians 5:18 again, particularly the phrase, "be filled with the Spirit." Notice the grammatical construction and verb tense.

Q How does the wording of this verse suggest that the "filling of the Spirit" is a divine work?

A _"be" with "filled" indicates a command to allow filling from another source_

Q How does the wording of Ephesians 5:18 also imply human responsibility in being "filled with the Spirit"?

A *a decision must be made to be filled"— a person must allow it*

The phrase "be filled" is in the *passive voice.* The passive voice means you are the recipient of another's action. Someone else takes the initiative and fills you. That someone is God Himself. Thus the command is *not* "fill yourself up with the Spirit," but rather, "*be* filled with the Spirit," implying that it is a divine work.

The other side of the coin is seen in the imperative mood of the verb. It is a straightforward command, not an optional extra for believers. The imperative mood demands obedience, implying choices and action on our part. Galatians 6:8 says, "The one who sows to his own flesh will from the flesh reap corruption, but the one who *sows to the Spirit* will from the Spirit reap eternal life" (emphasis added). The phrase "sows to the Spirit" suggests human responsibility.

Renowned devotional writer Richard Foster refers to this verse in his discussion of the divine and human roles in the process of spiritual development. He agrees that this verse suggests human responsibility but points out that our actions "only get us to the place where something can be done."[2]

Whether or not you apply the remaining content of this chapter to your own life depends on your grasp of this truth. Don't sit idly and expect a "holy zap" that results in a Spirit-filled Christian life. And on the other hand, don't perceive a Spirit-filled status as the sole result of some mechanical, human endeavor. View the following tips as means of obeying the command of Ephesians 5:18, of letting the Holy Spirit fill you. *Implementing these suggestions is simply a way of revealing to God a willing heart, thus allowing Him to do the filling.*

Sowing to the Spirit

What follows are several strategies for sowing to the Spirit and facilitating His work in your life.

Forsake Sin

Q Look up Psalm 32:1-5, and First John 1:9. By implication, what is one prerequisite for experiencing the fullness of the Holy Spirit?

A *Acknowledging and confessing sin to God, asking and receiving forgiveness and cleansing*

One way to sow to the Spirit is <u>an ongoing habit of confessing sin.</u> The briefer the time lapse between our awareness of a sin and a prayer of confession, the healthier we are spiritually. "To confess" means "to agree with," or "to say the same thing as." It means agreeing with God's perception of our sin rather than rationalizing it or treating it too casually. To our prayers of confession we must add a turning away from sin. When we genuinely view it from His perspective, we loathe sin and throw away the shackles it has placed on us. According to Jack Taylor,

> The teaching of many on the Holy Spirit is deficient because little or nothing is made of cleansing and its prerequisite, confession. Many a believer has been kept from the fullness of the Spirit by an unconfessed sin of such little proportion, humanly speaking, that one would be apt to pass over it.[3]

Sometimes you're conscious of a sin the instant you transgress. Others come to light as you prayerfully reflect on recent conversations, decisions and actions. During your quiet time reserve a brief chunk of time for confession. Review the past twenty-four hours and give the Holy Spirit permission to expose sins of thoughts and motives as well as behavior.

Right now, pause and ask the Lord to expose any unconfessed sin in your life. Ask Him to soften your heart so you start seeing sin from His perspective.

If you are to experience the Spirit's fullness you must get rid of all of the sin in your life—regardless of how small. The Holy Spirit and sin do not mix. Confess it, forsake it, be done with it.

Invite Christ to Be Lord

The next step you must take to be filled with the Holy Spirit is to <u>invite Christ to be in full, total and complete control of your life</u>. It's one thing to deal with your sins through confession, but it is quite another when you must deal with self, that is, the flesh or the source of these sins. <u>By inviting Christ to be Lord of your life, you make a conscious choice for Him to rule every facet of your life: your time, abilities, resources, future—the whole nine yards</u>. That's what Peter was calling for when he said, "<u>sanctify Christ as Lord in your hearts</u>" (1 Peter 3:15). The verb "sanctify" means "to set apart," or "to acknowledge."

Long, drawn-out battles between opposing forces often occur in war. But eventually one army wears down the other until the depleted band of soldiers raises a white flag denoting surrender. <u>A prayer of surrender is your way of raising a white flag and submitting to the rule of a new authority</u>. Andrew Murray put it like this: "<u>Our own life must be utterly cast aside to make full room for the life of God</u>."[4] Here's how Hannah Smith put it: "<u>We mean an entire surrender of the whole being to God—spirit, soul, and body placed under His absolute control, for Him to do just as He pleases</u>."[5] This step is hardly easy because "accepting the Lordship of Christ and thus the fullness of the Holy Spirit means nothing less than <u>the acceptance of death to the self-life</u>."[6] And self never wants to die. Self thinks he and only he knows what is best for him. James McConkey wrote,

> We may be assured that a step which the self-life supremely opposes is the supreme step the Spirit would have us take. That point at which the Flesh masses its most desperate resistance must be the point to which the Spirit is most desirous of bringing us.[7]

The irony is that only through no-strings-attached surrender can we experience true freedom and joy. That's because our Ruler is benevolent enough to have died on a cross for our sins!

Q Are you ready to "raise a white flag" and stage an initial surrender to God's control? If so, **write what you want to say to Him in the space provided.**

A *I have done this, Lord, and you have filled me, but with each stage or change in life I must do it again and again. "I must daily take up my cross"— Here and now, I do it again knowing that to be filled with your Spirit is the source of real abundant living.*

Look to God's Command

Many Bible teachers tell you to "invite Christ to be Lord," but they go no further. They assume that a one-time surrender to Christ's Lordship is sufficient for living a victorious Christian life.

An initial surrender is not enough. *Ongoing victory requires the Christian to be filled with the Spirit.* Escaping spiritual poverty and living the abundant Christian life involves not just living your life for God, but allowing Him to live His life through you. Or, as Philippians 2:13 says, "For it is God who is at work in you, both to will and to work for His good pleasure." God never intended for you to live the Christian life in your own efforts. That is why He tells you, commands you to let the Holy Spirit fill you. He knows you live in victory only through His enabling power. When you regularly look to God's command you realize that being Spirit-filled isn't some fancy accessory for the followers of Christ, but a vital necessity for dynamic Christian living.

Lean on God's Promises

Living a Spirit-filled life is a possibility for you— not an impossible dream—but the only way to achieve it is *by faith.*

The necessity of faith has been emphasized by numerous Bible teachers:

> Living in the Spirit means that I *trust* the Holy Spirit to do in me what I cannot do myself. . . . It is not a case of trying but of *trusting*; not of struggling but of resting in Him.[8]

—Watchman Nee

> In *faith* that God accepts my surrender and bestows this blessing upon me, I appropriate it for myself.[9]

—Andrew Murray

Here is another Christian who for years perhaps, has been seeking God's highest for him. He cares nothing for the world, nor the things of the world. He is utterly surrendered, to the point perhaps of legalism in giving up things perfectly legitimate. But he has never understood the simplicity of the step of *faith*.[10]

—Robertson C. McQuilkin

Many miss the fullness of the Spirit on a technicality. They do not *believe*.[11]

—Jack Taylor

[God] can bestow it only upon the fully consecrated soul, and that is to be received by *faith*.[12]

—Hannah W. Smith

Now God will certainly [work] through every life that is yielded to Him, if we simply *trust* Him so to do, and follow Him as He leads us on.[13]

—James H. McConkey

What are the conditions of this Victorious Life? Only two, and they are very simple. Surrender and *faith*. Let go and let God.[14]

—Charles S. Trumbull

. . . only those who meet God's requirements of personal dedication to His will and obedient *faith* are Spirit-filled.[15]

—Robert Witty

It is common for a young Christian to believe that he must rely on his own wisdom and strength to fight sin in his life, or to undertake some task God has given him. Such a person may realize that his salvation is based totally on what God has done in Christ, but at the same time be unaware that he is just as *dependent* on God the Holy Spirit for his Christian growth.[16]

—Billy Graham

Paul wrote, "As you therefore have received Christ Jesus the Lord, so walk in Him" (Colossians 2:6). How did you receive Christ? By *faith* in His provision for your sins. How do you receive the filling of the Holy Spirit? By *faith* in His promised provision of supernatural strength. Unfortunately, like the Christians in the third chapter of Galatians, many have, as Robertson McQuilkin said, "never understood the simplicity of the step of faith." If you want to escape spiritual poverty, you must trust God to live His life through you.

Q What is keeping you from trusting the Holy Spirit to live the life of Christ through you? Why?

A *Paralysis of analysis*

Express Your Desire for the Spirit's Filling

The next step to becoming filled with the Holy Spirit is the application of the two previous steps.

Since His filling is commanded, and since the Spirit's filling is appropriated by faith, you exercise your faith by expressing your desire for God to fill you. *He promises to give the Spirit's filling to everyone who asks for it.* In your quest for a Spirit-controlled life, lean on the following promise: "If you then, being evil, know how to give good gifts to your children, how much more will your heavenly Father give the Holy Spirit to those who ask Him?" (Luke 11:13).

If you are tired of living in spiritual poverty then pray, "God, I have sinned. I'm sorry, please forgive me. Lord Jesus, I turn myself over to You. I want You to control me, not myself. God, You have commanded me to be filled with the Spirit. You promised You would live Your life through me. Father God, I want You to do that. Will You fill me with Your Holy Spirit so I can begin right now to become the Christian You have created me to be?"

Here's a prayer Charles Swindoll often says as he sits on the side of his bed in the morning:

> This is Your day, Lord. I want to be at Your disposal. I have no idea what these next twenty-four hours will contain. But before I begin, before I sip my first cup of coffee, and even before I get dressed, I want You to know that from this moment on throughout this day, I'm Yours, Lord. . . . So I'm saying, Lord, fill me with Your Spirit today.[17]

Copy for my prayer book.

Please understand that a prayer like one of the above is more for your benefit than God's. His Holy Spirit will fill you as soon as you are clean, surrendered and trusting Him to do so. Praying simply helps you solidify in your heart what is happening.

 Write in your own words your desire to be filled with the Holy Spirit.

Fill me that I may be your woman in whatever circumstance I find myself.

Decide to Live by Faith, Instead of Feelings

Don't confuse faith and feelings. Trusting God day by day for the Spirit's filling is not an emotional experience. Yielding to His control—to His filling—isn't usually accompanied by feeling. So when you ask Him to fill you, keep this realistic perspective in mind: your faith is rooted in historical fact. What Christ did for you on the cross, plus what God has said in His Word, is your basis for trusting Him. Whereas God's reliability never fluctuates, human feelings vacillate from day to day. Bank on the following statement: "Faith must believe God in the entire absence of feeling or evidence. For God's Word is safer, better, and surer than any evidence or feeling. And remember that Christ Himself is better than any of His blessings, better than the power, or the victory, or the service that He grants."[18]

Q What are the dangers of seeking an emotional experience?

A *Discouragement, doubt when you are "down"*

Are your still living in spiritual poverty? Do you long to escape? If so, then follow the six steps discussed in this chapter and experience the victorious Christian life God has made available to you.

The Heart of the Matter

In this chapter, you have identified biblical information and concrete strategies to expedite your experience of the Holy Spirit's filling. Here is an easy way to remember the six steps. The first letter of each strategy forms the word FILLED.

How can you be "filled with the Spirit"?

- ✓ Forsake sin
- ✓ Invite Christ to be Lord
- ✓ Look to God's command
- ✓ Lean on God's promise
- ✓ Express your desire for the Spirit's filling
- ✓ Decide to live by faith instead of feelings

Right now, put a check mark by the steps you've already taken, or that you're in the process of applying. Put a "W" (for "willing") by any step that doesn't describe your current experience, but which you plan to implement.

Keep in mind that God looks upon your *heart*, not just your actions. What you do to apply this chapter is simply a way of revealing a hunger for Him. <u>When God sees a willing and hungry heart, He will fill it with the Holy Spirit</u>.

Memorizing Scripture

Tuck Luke 11:13 into the folds of your mind.

"If you then, though you are evil, know how to give good gifts to your children, how much more will your Father in heaven give the Holy Spirit to those who ask him!"

[margin handwritten note: A prayer that never turns down.]

The command to "be filled" (Ephesians 5:18) is in the present tense. It is a continuous appropriation, not some great, high-and-mighty, once-in-a-lifetime moment where you experience the fullness of the Spirit and from then on you are on an all-time high that never wanes.[1]

—Charles Swindoll

How Can I Walk in the Holy Spirit?

The following truth is a sobering, profound realization: *There's only one thing worse than being a sinner. And that's not being aware of it.*

This maxim equates a continual awareness of our proneness to sin with spiritual health. It suggests that a Christian who understands his potential to sin is more likely to persist in spiritual disciplines and to resist temptation.

Bull's-eye! A sensitivity to the relentless spiritual warfare during your earthly pilgrimage keeps you alert and sober. You are less likely to turn to the devil's temptation or the sinful desires within you. The need to "guard your heart" (Proverbs 4:23, NIV) on a daily basis is the rationale for this chapter on walking in the Spirit. You may start your day filled with the Holy Spirit but within a few hours, attacks of the world, the flesh and the devil can penetrate your defenses, resulting in a grieving or a quenching of the Holy Spirit. Chapter 8 offered initial strategies for experiencing the Spirit's fullness. This chapter on walking in the Spirit suggests ways to *stay filled* throughout the day—to stay under the Holy Spirit's control.

Because you're aware that sinning is still a possibility, mull over the following perspectives and action plans.

Watch Out for the Flesh

We have examined the characteristics of human nature apart from the control of God's Spirit, a state which Paul called "walk[ing] according to the flesh" (see Romans 8:4-8), or yielding to "deeds of the flesh" (see Galatians 5:19-21).

It is necessary to cultivate a constant vigil against the selfish bent of your human nature because asking God to fill you with His Spirit each morning is not, in itself, a sufficient battle strategy. Even after you prayerfully surrender your day to the Lord, Satan works in tandem with the flesh in an effort to usurp the Spirit's control over you.

Look up the following mandates for vigilant Christian living.

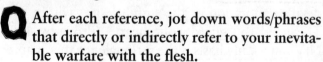 After each reference, jot down words/phrases that directly or indirectly refer to your inevitable warfare with the flesh.

A Romans 13:14: *thoughts about how to gratify the desires of my sinful nature arise all the time—"My mind takes me there."*

A First Peter 1:13-15: *prepare minds self-control, trust grace, obedient to holy—flesh, world, + devil will fight these continually.*

A First Peter 2:11: *"sinful desires war against your soul."*

Next, lock your mental lens on First John 2:16: "For all that is in the world, the lust of the flesh and the lust of the eyes and the boastful pride of life, is not from the Father, but is from the world." How does "the lust of the eyes" express itself? <u>By wanting to possess what God does not want you to have.</u> What constitutes "the lust of the flesh"? <u>Wanting to engage in what God does not want you to do.</u> How does "the boastful pride of life" show? <u>In wanting to be what God does not want you to be.</u>

A story featuring King Saul in First Samuel 15 demonstrates the enticements and working of the flesh. Read First Samuel 15 slowly, digesting every word, paying special attention to the words, actions and motives of King Saul. Also note what is said about the people of Amalek. When you finish this narrative, go back and delve into specific verses in order to answer the following questions.

Q 1. 15:1-3. What can you learn about God from His response to the Amalekites' deeds of the flesh?

A As a holy God, He will punish sin.

Q 2. 15:10-12. What indicates that Saul was "walking in the flesh" rather than "walk[ing] in the Spirit"?

A Did not follow God's instructions. set up monument to honor himself

Q 3. Compare the content of 15:13-14 with God's command in 15:3. How did Saul exhibit self-deception?

A He saved the best instead of killing all thinking (rationalizing) he could present them as offering to Lord. The Lord couldn't want best "killed"

Q 4. 15:15-21. What evidences of "walking in the flesh" do you see here?

A Blamed soldiers for decision to keep best. taking no personal responsibility for own sin of disobedience

Q 5. In what ways do people today try to rationalize or justify sinful behavior?

have thought he did a better plan than God.

A _Blaming others; pleading ignorance; running away; denial; having a better plan; compromise; cover with "religious activity"_

Q 6. 15:22 implies that some people try to compensate for deeds of the flesh by engaging in religious activities. **Why is religious duty never a substitute for obedience?**

A _God looks upon the heart first. unless the heart is right before God, religious activity is meaningless_

Q 7. What truth about "walking in the flesh" does 15:23-29 suggest?

A _It is based in rebellion and pride and rejection of God's Word. Just like divination and idolatry._

Q 8. Look at 15:32-35. Some Bible scholars view the Amalekites as a symbol or picture of human nature controlled by fleshly desires. Consequently, the attitude God had toward the people of Amalek in First Samuel 15 would represent His attitude toward deeds of the flesh. **With that in mind, what does Samuel's treatment of King Agag suggest about how to treat our sinful nature?**

A _We need to "kill the deeds of the flesh" before and in the name of the Lord._

Jerry Bridges offers an analogy that vividly illustrates the internal tug-of-war between the desires of the flesh and the desires of the Spirit. He explains why a Christian isn't immune to the pull of fleshly desires.

> Two competing factions were fighting for control of [a] country. . . . One faction won the war and assumed control of the nation's government. But the losing side did not stop fighting. They simply changed their tactics to guerrilla warfare and continued to fight. . . .
>
> So it is with the Christian. Satan has been defeated and the reign of sin overthrown. But the sinful nature resorts to a sort of guerrilla warfare to lead us into sin.[2]

Many Christians forget how much God despises the flesh and for one reason or another tend to drift back into the flesh. Sometimes the reason is quite noble. They simply want to be godly but they are striving for holiness in their own strength and effort. Andrew Murray writes,

> There are Christians who begin with the Spirit but end with the flesh. They are converted, born again through the Spirit, but fall unconsciously into a life in which they endeavor to overcome sin and be holy through their own exertion, through doing their best. They ask God to help them in their endeavors and think that this is faith.[3]

The Christian life must always be received by faith in the Spirit, not achieved by works of the flesh. So regardless of your motivations, watch out for the flesh trying to creep back into your practice.

In order to walk continually in the fullness of God's Spirit, one must constantly be on the lookout for the flesh exerting its ugly influence. A temporary neglect of vigilance will allow the sinful nature to reexert itself and take you once again down the path of spiritual poverty.

Attend to Your Heart's Inner Fire

A second step toward victorious Christian living is *attending to your heart's inner fire*. In your study on quenching the Holy Spirit, you discovered that quench is a *fire* word. It means to dampen or to extinguish. This second strategy for walking in the Spirit calls for you to furnish fuel for the fire in your heart so its flame burns consistently rather than off and on.

The following illustration will help show how to feed the heart's fire. An elderly Eskimo fisherman came to town every weekend. He always brought two dogs with him. He had taught them to fight each other on command. Every Saturday afternoon, in the town square, folks gathered to watch the two dogs fight. They would place bets with the fisherman on which dog would win. Neither dog dominated from week to week. After a couple wins by one dog, the other would win. Villagers could never be sure on a given day which mutt to bet on. Yet no matter which dog proved victor on a given day, the fisherman always won his bets and pocketed lots of cash. Away from the hearing range of the towns-people, a friend asked the fisherman how he managed to win every bet. What the dog owner said offers insight into spiritual warfare as well: "Each week I starve one dog and feed the other one. Because the dog I feed that week is so much stronger, he always wins!"[4]

Winning at spiritual warfare also requires energy. Fuel for your heart comes in the form of spiritual food. Consequently, Scripture is a vital part of your spiritual diet.

Following are some practical suggestions for attending to your heart's fire through biblical intake. Carefully read each strategy listed to determine which best satisfies your spiritual hunger. Implement one strategy for each of the three steps.

1. Read God's Word

- Read five psalms a day each month.
- Read one chapter a day from Proverbs, corresponding with the day of the month.
- Read one chapter of the New Testament each day.
- To finish the Bible in one year, read four chapters daily.

2. Study God's Word

- Outline one chapter each week.
- Get a study Bible and examine all the notes.

- Purchase a Bible study curriculum and work through it.

- Get a series of tapes from a Bible teacher and take notes as you listen.

- When you read a chapter or less for devotional purposes, jot down answers you find to the following questions:

  1. How does this passage increase my appreciation for God the Father, Jesus Christ or the Holy Spirit?

  2. What reasons for praising the Lord does the text offer?

  3. What sin to avoid or to forsake does the content expose?

  4. What bearing do these verses have on my prayer life?

  5. What encourages me from the passage? Why?

  6. What circumstances, decisions or people come to mind as I read? Why?

3. Memorize God's Word

- Select one verse each week that the Lord impresses on you.

- Try memorizing one psalm each month.

- Look for five verses on a topic.

- Select an appropriate memory verse to go over with your children and spouse.

A second source of fuel for your heart is prayer. The following strategies can fan the flame of your commitment.

- Write God a love letter citing specific reason for your love for Him.
- Before turning in for the night, pray with your spouse or roommate.
- Reserve a half day for extended communion with the Lord. Take a Bible, pen, notebook and hymnal to facilitate your interaction with Him.

Don't confine your participation in Bible study and prayer to private moments. You are a part of the body of Christ so your participation in a local church is also integral to a burning heart. Consider the following methods and try to implement at least one.

1. Study the Bible with other believers by attending a Sunday school class or launching a Bible study in your home.
2. Start a prayer/accountability group that meets weekly.
3. Look for a way to serve the Lord through one of your church's ministries.
4. Once a month, invite someone from church into your home after the Sunday worship service.

Perhaps another analogy will reinforce the importance of attending to your heart's inner fire. Picture a one-year-old child. Perhaps he can walk, but not very well. Often he stumbles and falls. As he grows older, he takes steps with more confidence and stability. During this child's early years, his ability to respond to his parents is limited. His attention span is short. He's too immature to understand all of their instructions. He's naturally self-centered, more sensitive to his own needs than to his folks' wishes. But as he grows, his physical, mental and emotional capacities expand. With increased age comes an increasing capacity to heed his parents' instructions, to focus on pleasing them rather than himself.

That's how it is with walking in the Holy Spirit. It's possible for a new or immature believer to be *filled* with the Spirit, but his walk may be inconsistent. He stumbles more often. And since he's so young in the faith, he's still more self-centered than God-centered in his thinking. He's limited in his capacity to focus on the Lord rather than his own needs. Only as he grows spiritually will his focus shift to what pleases God. Only as he increases communication with God, expands his understanding of Scripture and spends time with other Christians will his commitment solidify. There's a flicker of fire in his heart the moment he becomes a Christian, but the more consistently he fuels that fire, the bigger and hotter the flames get.

Q In your own words, explain why a life of walking in the Holy Spirit isn't automatic once you're filled with the Spirit.

A *Because we fight the world, flesh, and devil in order*

*to be obedient God's Spirit.
Plus, "Christ's life" – the Christian
life – is lived in & through us
by the Holy Spirit, not by our
self efforts*

Q Complete the following sentence: **One way I'm going to start attending to my heart's inner fire is:**

A *Morning & evening prayer
including confession and
scripture reading/study.*

Listen to Inner Promptings

So far you've identified two broad strategies for "walking in the Spirit": _watch out for the flesh_ and _attend to your heart's inner fire_. A third principle is to _listen to inner promptings_.

In a previous chapter titled "How Do I Quench the Holy Spirit?" you were introduced to the concept of inner promptings. You learned that it refers to the "still small voice" of the Spirit—to subjective impressions He creates as a way of sending messages of peace, warning, conviction or guidance. You also discovered that inner promptings are *not* new revelations from God. What He impresses on you subjectively flows from—and will never contradict—what He has already revealed objectively in Scripture. It's a form of divine communication that we cannot nail down and dissect with precision. Yet we cannot deny its reality either.

Bill Bright, founder of Campus Crusade for Christ, had this to say on the significance of listening to inner promptings and testing those promptings in light of Scripture:

> When God seems to be telling me to undertake a specific project, I . . . test the impressions to see if it is from God or from Satan or my own thoughts. . . . I cannot stress enough the importance of getting to know and respond to the perfect, holy, sovereign mind of God through regular, Spirit-led study and application of His inspired Word.[5]

Q What inner prompting do you think God's Spirit has given you lately?

A *Serve as ESL instructor at LEC.*

Q How do you know this inner prompting is from the Holy Spirit, as opposed to your own flesh or Satan?

A *Has led me to train, given me experience, given me heart to do it, given me opportunity at EC*

All this units a growing conviction of serving the unchurched and poor.

When you believe that the Holy Spirit is prompting you, test its reliability with the following questions.

- Will what I'm prompted to do glorify God?
- Am I aware of any Bible truth or verse which contradicts or invalidates this inner prompting?

- Is my ability to interpret this prompting hindered by unconfessed sin in my life?

- Will what I'm prompted to do have an edifying effect on someone else or meet a legitimate need in someone's life?

- Is my ability to understand this inner prompting or to ascertain its source clouded by emotional involvement with someone? By physical exhaustion? By depression or discouragement? By physical illness? By long-standing desires of some sort?

- Do one or more Christians whom I respect give me feedback that contradicts this inner prompting?

- Am I being pushed to make a snap decision?

- Has God provided the resources I need for what I sense He is telling me to do?

- Have I asked God to solidify this inner prompting so I can be sure that it's from His Spirit?

Digest the following words with caution:

> As confident as I am that God speaks to me, I am equally confident that I have the potential to read my will into His. I am capable of misunderstanding God. For this reason, you will never hear me flaunting the fact that God spoke to me.[6]

God is big enough to communicate to you. As Romans 8:14 says, "For all who are being led by the Spirit of God, these are sons of God." If He lives in your life then you can be sensitive to those promptings by listening for any impressions of the Holy Spirit.

Keep on Being Filled

A full understanding of walking in the Spirit requires a review of a point made in Chapter 8. In Ephesians 5:18, the command "Be filled with the Spirit" is in the present tense. A literal rendering is, "*Keep on* being filled." The verb tense implies that His filling is a continual process, not a once-in-a-lifetime experience or event.

According to Paul Little,

> The filling of the Spirit is an experience to be repeated as necessary in the life of each believer. We are, literally, to "keep on being filled" (Ephesians 5:18). The fullness of the Spirit is not a matter of receiving more of Him. Rather, it is a matter of relationship.[7]

When you do grieve Him and blow it, spiritually speaking, you must be refilled by following the six steps studied in Chapter 8. This is not, however, to remain a mechanical routine. Neil Anderson says, "The moment you think you have reduced the Spirit-filled walk to a formula, it probably isn't Spirit-filled anymore."[8] This is so true. Walking in the fullness of the Spirit is a relationship, not a routine. Yet just like a beginning golfer thinks through the mechanics of his swing until it becomes natural, it is helpful initially to break walking in the Spirit into specific steps until it becomes part of your experience. As you become more acquainted with Spirit-filled Christian living, the six steps will melt into your heart's response expressed with words similar to the following:

> Father, I'm sorry I sinned against You. On the basis of Jesus' death for me on the cross, I ask You to forgive me. Jesus, once again take Your rightful place on the throne of my heart. Holy Spirit, rightly now, by faith, I appropriate Your fullness. Thank You for making me sensitive to sin, and for giving me the desire and the power to escape spiritual poverty. In Jesus' name, Amen.

Put in prayer books.

To escape spiritual poverty, it is not enough to rededicate your life to the lordship of Christ. God never meant for any man to live the Christian life by his own efforts. For Christ to live His life through you, you must be filled with the Spirit. But being filled with the Spirit is not an end in itself. Rather, it is a beginning. Many Christians have surrendered their self-life to Christ and have trusted God's Spirit to live His life through them only to end up in spiritual poverty again. To live the normal Christian life consistently you must walk in the Spirit.

To summarize, walking in the Spirit involves:

- Watching out for the influences of the flesh so you don't succumb to temptation. *(Watch out for the flesh.)*

- Attending to the spiritual fire of your heart in order that you might grow in spiritual maturity. *(Attend to your heart's inner fire.)*

- Listening for any promptings by the Holy Spirit so you can fulfill God's desires for your life. *(Listen to inner promptings.)*

- And finally, when you happen to grieve or quench the Spirit, allowing God to re-fill you so that you miss no more time than necessary living the Christian life He created you to live. *(Keep being filled.)*

To facilitate recollection of the four steps to walking in the Spirit, note that the first letters of the four italicized sentences spell W-A-L-K.

Q The most convicting or challenging insight from this chapter is:

A *"Watch out for flesh"- confession*

Q The most encouraging or reassuring truth in this chapter is:

A *God is gracious, and will fill me when I empty myself in faith before Him.*

Q The point from this chapter that will have the most bearing on my immediate behavior is:

A Confession and vigilence especially in my attitude toward my husband.

Memorizing Scripture

Reflect on Galatians 5:16-18 until you can recite it from memory.

"So I say, live by the Spirit, and you will not gratify the desires of the sinful nature. For the sinful nature desires what is contrary to the Spirit, and the Spirit what is contrary to the sinful nature. They are in conflict with each other, so that you do not do what you want to do. But if you are led by the Spirit, you are not under the law."

There is a great market for religious experience in our world; there is little enthusiasm for the patient acquisition of virtue, little inclination to sign up for a long apprenticeship in what earlier generations of Christians called holiness.[1]

—Eugene Peterson

How Can I Exhibit the Fruit of the Holy Spirit?

H.G. Spafford lost his business in the great Chicago fire. Then he sent his wife and four daughters back to France aboard a ship. A mid-Atlantic collision sunk the ship. Only a few passengers were rescued, including Mrs. Spafford. She sent a cable back to her husband in the United States, containing only two words: "Saved alone." All four daughters had perished. Mr. Spafford took a passenger ship to Europe to join his wife. While grieving for his daughters as he crossed the Atlantic, he wrote the beloved hymn, "It Is Well with My Soul."[2] Notice how the lyrics reveal his incredible faith in eternal outcomes, even while he experienced heartache.

It Is Well with My Soul

When peace like a river attendeth my way,
When sorrows like sea billows roll,
Whatever my lot, Thou hast taught me to say,
"It is well, it is well with my soul."

It is well with my soul;
it is well, it is well, with my soul!

Though Satan should buffet, though trials
  should come,
Let this blest assurance control,
That Christ hath regarded my helpless estate,
And hath shed His own blood for my soul.

My sin—oh, the bliss of this glorious thought—
My sin, not in part but the whole,
Is nailed to His cross and I bear it no more!
Praise the Lord, praise the Lord, O my soul!

And, Lord, haste the day when the faith shall
  be sight,
The clouds be rolled back as a scroll,
The trump shall resound, and the Lord shall
  descend!
Even so—it is well, with my soul.[3]

Spafford's peace in the midst of pain was possible only because the Holy Spirit controlled him. He exhibited what is called the fruit of the Holy Spirit. As you learn to walk in the Spirit, you will express the reality of His involvement in your life. This is the first of three studies on how walking in the Spirit expresses itself. After this lesson on the fruit of the Spirit, you will survey the *gifts* of the

Spirit, then you will examine the *power* of the Holy Spirit.

What Is the "Fruit of the Spirit"?

Over the centuries there have been well-meaning Christians who, out of a desire for holiness, practiced various lifestyles ranging from the curious to the bizarre. For example,

> An Egyptian named Anthony, disturbed because Christians no longer seemed to have a self-sacrificing spirit, sold his family possessions and fled to the wilderness. Anthony ate once a day, and only bread and salt and water. He never again changed his clothes or washed his face, and he died at the age of 105.
>
> Monasticism (at a later date) came to be seen as the best path to holiness, and deprivation was built into the monastic life. The Abbot Dioscorus was an early advocate of making New Year's resolutions. Once he vowed not to speak for a year, another year he swore off cooked food, another he vowed not to meet anyone. He kept all these resolutions.
>
> Some of the feats of hermits and monks were amazing. Self-flagellation—whipping one's flesh to imitate Christ's wounds—was common. The famous Simeon Stylites chose to live for thirty-seven years atop a pillar among ruins. A group called the Dendrites lived in trees, basing the practice on a verse in James about keeping oneself unspotted from the world.[4]

Though Christians today do not pursue such extreme measures to become holy, they might be just as misguided. As mentioned in the last chapter, even worthwhile pursuits like Scripture reading, prayer and church attendance are useless if done in the flesh. Without the Spirit's fullness, they advance one's spiritual growth about as effectively as living in a tree.

Like many Christians before you, you may have believed that if you worked hard enough at overcoming a sin, then one day you could become a godly person. That is not, however, the way holiness is achieved. Jesus did more than just die on the cross for your sins. He sent the Holy Spirit to enable you to live the victorious Christian life.

During the early days of spring you may see dead, brown leaves on some trees that didn't fall to the ground in autumn. Those stubborn leaves clung to the tree limbs through the cold winds and snows of winter. But you don't bother to climb those trees and pluck the lackluster leaves by hand because you know that warmer weather will invigorate the branches and launch the process of new growth. The spring sap will propel new life through the limbs and push off the dead leaves.

The working of the Holy Spirit in your life is similar to this natural process. The inner presence of the Holy Spirit warms your heart, serving as a catalyst for growth. As you tap into His power through obedience, His presence magnifies itself and exerts more and more influence. Gradually the Spirit generates Christlike character that expels sinful habits—those "dead leaves" that marked your lifestyle prior to conversion. Galatians 5:22-23 lists the qualities that take the place of those dead leaves: "But the fruit of the Spirit is love, joy, peace, patience, kindness, goodness, faithfulness, gentleness, self-control; against such things there is no law."

Let's put each fruit of the Spirit under a mental microscope.

Love

The Greek term for "love" in Galatians 5:22 is *agape*. It's the kind of love that God demonstrates: selfless, sacrificial and unconditional. The word connotes love rooted in commitment, not just feeling or some form of natural attraction. When the Holy Spirit controls a person, it's possible to exercise that kind of love in a human sphere.

An employee at Boston's New England Medical Center observed a distinguished-looking gentleman and his young son. They visited daily over a period of time as the boy received treatments in the cancer ward. Not only did the man wear tailored suits each day, but he also stood out due to a head of lush gray hair that was impeccably groomed. During one particular visit, the employee noticed that the cap usually worn by the boy was missing, revealing a shiny, bald head. Then her eyes shifted to the father, who was as bald as his son. "Look at my dad!" exclaimed the boy. "He shaved his head so we could look the same. We're going to grow our hair back together." The boy's father smiled at the employee. To her, the

man seemed more distinguished than ever. That's
agape love![5]

Q Look up First Corinthians 13:4-7. **What are some characteristics of *agape* love?**

A *patient, kind, not envious not boastful, not proud, not rude, not self-seeking, not easily angered, keeps no records of wrongs, hates evil, rejoices in truth, protects, trusts, hopes, perseveres*

Q Probe John 13:34-35. **According to Jesus, why is this kind of extraordinary love for others important?**

A *So that others will recognize you belong to Jesus.*

Q Think of a relationship you have with some-one that is lacking this kind of sacrificial love. If you exhibited agape love in this rela-tionship, how would it show?

A _____

_____

_____

Remember: you can't conjure up this type of
love through your own willpower. Since it is not
natural to express this form of love, its source is
supernatural—the Holy Spirit. It's possible only
when you trust the Spirit of God to change you
and to love others through you.

Ask Him to do just that in the relationship you cited above.

"In spite of it all, there is a deep sense of joy..."

Joy

How is *joy* different from *happiness*? Someone has said that "even when your happenings don't happen to happen the way you happen to want your happenings to happen, you can still be joyful!"[6] Translated, that means happiness depends on positive, favorable outward circumstances. Joy, however, comes from positive, favorable, inward circumstances. It is an inward trait, rooted in eternal values and perspectives rather than external conditions. As you yield daily to the Holy Spirit's control, He instills within you joy, not just happiness.

When I (Terry) was in high school, the Friday night football games were a highlight to me. Win or lose, I rooted for our team enthusiastically from the bleachers. Then in my senior year, I got my first pair of eyeglasses. I had not realized just how poor my eyesight was until I attended a football game and I could actually see the numbers on the players' jerseys. All along I had assumed that no one could see the numbers from the stands. What a different perspective on the game those glasses provided!

Similarly, the Holy Spirit can give you a better view of even adverse circumstances. Despite the pain, He can give you an eternal perspective on things. You view life through lenses provided by the Spirit—and it makes a big difference in what you see and how well you see. For the first time, you en-

joy things from <u>God's perspective instead of your</u>
<u>own.</u>

Q Digest John 15:11. **What was Jesus' goal for His followers?**

A *That we would experience his joy, and that our joy would be complete*

Q Now skim John 15:1-10. **What condition did Jesus give for experiencing His joy?**

A *Abiding as a branch in Him as the vine so that His sources can produce fruit — joy — in our lives*

Q To what extent are you experiencing this joy? **Explain.**

A *In spite of my physical pain, and emotional pain, I do experience a sense of joy that I know can only come*
Peace *from God.*

The Bible discusses peace *with* God, as well as the peace *of* God. <u>Peace *with* God refers to the benefit</u>
<u>of salvation. It's your new status with God. You are</u>
<u>no longer His enemy.</u> Because Jesus paid the penalty for your sins, you are now a full-fledged member of God's family. But you must keep in mind that peace *with* God doesn't guarantee that you'll experience th<u>e peace *of*</u> God. This fruit of the Holy Spirit refers to a sense of order, rest or security inside a

person. Like the trait of joy, God's peace is possible even in the context of frustrating circumstances on the outside.

Q Lock your mental lens on Philippians 4:6-7. What is one means of experiencing this fruit of the Holy Spirit?

A *Surrendering anxiety in prayers of thanksgiving, petition in every circumstances.*

Q How did Paul describe this kind of peace?

A *transcends understanding guards heart and minds*

Right now, jot down three sources of anxiety—three hindrances to experiencing the peace of God in your life.

1. *marital relationship present & future*
2. *pain, health issues present & future*
3. *money/finances for future*

Q In view of these threatening circumstances, to what extent are you currently experiencing the peace that "surpasses all comprehension" (Philippians 4:7)?

A *Inconsistently —.*

Seek the Lord in prayer concerning the needs you have identified.

Remember that peace isn't something you generate through self-effort. It's a quality cultivated by the Holy Spirit, so <u>keep your focus on the *Giver* of peace,</u> not the trait itself. Here's how Charles H. Spurgeon put it: "<u>I looked at Christ and the dove of peace flew into my heart. I looked at the dove of peace and it flew away.</u>"[7]

Patience

You have no doubt heard what's known as the typical "American" prayer: *"Lord, give me patience—and hurry!"*

In Western culture, patience is an almost extinct trait. It's on the endangered species list of virtues because impatience is a mark of our culture. We're used to everything from microwaves to e-mail, from fast-food drive-through windows to "call waiting." When we're stuck in a traffic jam or put on hold over the phone, we get irritable.

<u>Patience is a Christlike quality that suggests the ability to wait without getting edgy; to persevere when outcomes don't develop as soon as we expected. It's a fruit of the Spirit</u> grounded in trust, especially when God's timing is different than our wishes.

Q Reflect on the words in Psalm 27:13-14. What divine attribute did David link to the capacity to wait?

A _confidence in God to bring good out of circumstances_

Q Mull over Lamentations 3:25. **What is God's response to the person who "seeks Him" during times of delay?**

A _He is good!_

Perhaps you're between jobs and waiting for that call from a prospective employer. Perhaps your trek to a mission field has been delayed due to a lack of funds. Perhaps you are wondering when God is going to answer your prayer for a husband or wife. Situations of this sort call for dependence upon God, and trust in His timing. V. Raymond Edman wrote, "Delay never thwarts God's purposes. It merely polishes His instruments."[8]

Q Describe one area of your life where you're currently frustrated by delay or timing. How might God be wanting to "polish" you during this time?

A _My husband refuses to acknowledge he is married to me and refuses to go to church, pray, read God's word, serve others ever since his "midlife" crises. We separated; he left - he came back to sleep alone in the house - only._

Kindness

Words associated with kindness include "gracious," "considerate" and "benevolent." Kindness is a fruit of the Spirit that exerts life-changing influence on those who receive it.

Two farmers tilled their land on a terraced mountain in Japan. The owner of the higher plot of land was a Christian. During planting season, both men had to carry water up the hill and pour it into irrigation ditches. Then the farmer on the lower level figured out a way to water his soil without all the exertion. Each day, he poked a hole in the dike replenished with water by the farmer above him, releasing water that flowed downhill and soaked into his soil.

The Christian farmer considered revenge, but waited several days to see if the dishonest act continued. For three more days he lugged water to his property. And for three more days the farmer below him drained off the water to quench his own plot's thirst. The Christian man's crops were in the process of dying. He visited his pastor for advice and received unusual counsel. His pastor told him to water his neighbor's plot first, then proceed up the hill to water his own land. After observing this extraordinary kindness for three days, the Christian's neighbor paid him a visit. Then he said, "Please tell me how I can become a Christian."[9]

Q Read First Peter 2:2-3. **How has the Lord expressed His kindness toward you?**

A *Through giving his Son for my salvation*

Q Soak up the words of Micah 6:8. **What qualities go hand-in-glove with kindness?**

A *goodness, justice, mercy, walking humbly in fellowship with God*

Q Is kindness merely an ideal optional trait for a Christian? Why or why not? (Base your answer on Micah 6:8.)

A *It is a requirement. As a Christian, one pleases God to express His trait of kindness.*

Q Think of someone in your sphere of influence who could benefit from an act of kindness. Jot down his or her name, and what you could do to demonstrate kindness this week.

A *Bernarda - a ride home with her groceries, giving her books she needs*

Goodness

Goodness is a basic attribute of God, representing the highest possible moral and ethical value.

The Bible apparently esteems goodness even
more than righteousness. Notice how Paul ele-
vated a "good" man over a "righteous" man: "For
one will hardly die for a righteous man; though
perhaps for the good man someone would dare
even to die" (Romans 5:7).

A righteous person is a law-keeper. In one sense
even the Pharisees were righteous, due to their
meticulous external compliance with God's law.
But goodness goes beyond compliance with law:
It refers to a state of being, to an inner force of
character marked by pure motives and a clean
heart. A good person is concerned with far more
than just the letter of the law.

Q Focus your attention on Romans 15:13-14.
When the Holy Spirit cultivates goodness
within you, what consequence does it have?

A *You will have complete knowledge,*
hope, power and competency
to instruct one another.

Q From God's perspective, to what extent are
you a "good" person? How do you rate your
goodness? Why?

A *If good = godly. I am good*
to the extent I have let
the Lord impact my life, and
He has in many ways.

Even an unbeliever occasionally performs
deeds that are labeled "good." But goodness as a
habit of character, consistently spawned by un-

selfish motives, is impossible apart from the Holy Spirit's mastery of a person. Here is Francis Bacon's salute to goodness: "Of all virtues and dignities of the mind, goodness is the greatest, being the character of the Deity. For without it man is a busy, mischievous and wretched thing."[10]

Faithfulness

This fruit of the Spirit isn't faith *in* God, but a faithfulness *before* God. The term describes someone who doesn't waver in his loyalty to God. He doesn't quit or shirk his duty to God when the going gets rough. Synonyms include responsible, dependable and consistent over time in relation to God and His values. It is *spiritual stick-to-itiveness!*

An ancient Persian legend illustrates the trait of faithfulness. A king, searching for a faithful servant, narrowed the choice to two men. Before choosing the person for this privileged position, he told both men to go to a well, and get the water with a bucket, then pour each bucketful into a basket full of tiny holes. The king did not give a reason for the strange instruction. Of course, the water always spilled from the basket onto the ground.

Before long, one servant exclaimed, "This is foolish! What's the point of pouring water into a basket with holes?" The other servant replied, "It doesn't matter. We're doing the king's business, exactly the way he told us to do it. We're receiving our wages, so why complain?" Yet the first servant flung his bucket and stomped off, refusing to do what he perceived as nonsense. The other servant kept at it for hours until he had emptied the entire well. Then at the bottom, stuck in the mud, he spotted a shiny object. He scraped the bottom with his bucket and hauled in a large diamond ring.

Then the rationale for pouring the water through a leaky basket hit him. If they had scooped up the ring in the process of emptying the well, they might have thrown away the diamond along with the muddy water, without ever seeing it. But by pouring it through a basket that served as a sieve, the ring would have stayed in the basket while the water escaped.

Faithfulness to God means obeying when it's difficult or when His way of life looks ludicrous from the world's viewpoint. God sees the big picture; we don't.

Q Look closely at First Corinthians 1:9. **What serves as an impetus for your faithfulness to God?**

A *God is our witness.*

Q Describe a time when you experienced God's faithfulness to you.

A *Comfort, perfect timing in death of my father from cancer.*

Think of one area in your spiritual life—perhaps one in which obedience has become routine and boring—in which God is calling you to *stick-to-itiveness*.

Q If you demonstrated loyalty to God in this area, how would it show?

A *I will continue to be the best wife I can be, whether I am loved, or not.*

Gentleness

Gentleness is *strength under control*. Rather than suggesting weakness or timidity or a spineless approach to people, it connotes a mild, soothing manner even in a heated atmosphere. Charles Swindoll tells how extra-biblical usage of this Greek term enhances our understanding of it.

- A wild stallion that has been tamed, brought under control, is described as being "gentle."

- Carefully chosen words that soothe strong emotions are referred to as "gentle."

- In one of Plato's works, a child asks the physician to be tender as he treats him. The child uses the term "gentle."

- Ointment that takes the fever and sting out of a wound is called "gentle."

- Those who are polite, who have tact and are courteous, and who treat others with dignity and respect are called "gentle" people.[11]

Q Who do you associate with the trait of gentleness? Why?

A *Kathy; she is all the above.*

Q What effect does a lack of gentleness have on relationships?

A *Destroy them by hurting others verbally, emotionally socially, and spiritually*

Q Specifically, <u>how</u> does the Lord want you to express gentleness among family members?

A *Soothe emotions with gentle words - mother, Ruth, Judy, Jact courtesy, respect, dignity with Bob. With children - to build*

Q Among associates at work or school? *up.*

A *Jact, courtesy, respect, dignity.*

According to Matthew 11:29, Jesus was "gentle and humble in heart." Romans 8:29 asserts that God's goal for you has always been conformity to "the image of His Son." Gentleness can characterize *you* if you rely on God's Spirit for its cultivation.

Self-Control

The word translated "self-control" carries the idea of "getting a grip on" or "taking hold" of something. It's the capacity to govern your thoughts and actions wisely.

For a Christian, self-control is integral to maturity in these five areas at the least:

1. *Thought life*.

> If you sow a thought, you reap an attitude.
> If you sow an attitude, you reap an action.
> If you sow an action, you reap a habit.
> If you sow a habit, you reap a character.[12]

Those anonymous lines are called "the law of the harvest." They reveal the ultimate consequences of your thoughts.

Q Look up Philippians 4:8. **What are some characteristics of a Spirit-controlled thought life?**

A *True, noble, right, pure, lovely, admirable, excellent, praiseworthy*

2. *Money*. Money is a wonderful servant, but a horrible master. Scripture suggests that how we handle material resources is the leading indicator of whether or not we love God! Sixteen out of the thirty-eight parables Jesus taught deal with money. More is said in the New Testament about money than heaven and hell combined. Five times more is said about money than prayer—so it's an important issue to God![13]

Self-control in the spending of money reflects an eternal rather than a temporal value system, and enables us to give more to the work of God in the world.

Q According to First Timothy 6:7, what factor should impel us to develop self-control over money?

A *We won't take it with us, and we didn't bring it with us.*

3. *Time.* Few of us allow other people to control our money but we often allow others to dictate how we spend our time—a commodity that's even more valuable. How we use our time reflects our value system and purpose in life. How we spend this limited resource has eternal consequences. Paul's first-century advice to the Ephesian believers is just as appropriate for us: "Be careful how you walk, not as unwise men, but as wise, making the most of your time, because the days are evil" (Ephesians 5:15-16).

4. *Eating habits.* Like sexual lust, overindulgence in food is slavery to a physical appetite. Whether or not bodily weight is a problem, gluttony, as well as eating unhealthy foods, has a negative impact on energy and longevity as well as our witness to others. Eating disorders such as bulimia and anorexia may spring from a value system that exalts external features, showing a disastrous lack of a proper value system.

5. _Tongue_. Jesus didn't mince words when He said a man's "mouth speaks from that which fills his heart" (Luke 6:45). That's a way of saying that an accurate gauge of spirituality is the nature of our daily conversations. Proverbs 18:21 insists that words have an awesome capacity to hurt as well as to help: "Death and life are in the power of the tongue."

Q Examine Ephesians 4:29. **What practical guidelines for daily conversation does this verse offer?**

A _Speak only what builds up, meets needs individually, and benefits all who listen._

Q Evaluate your self-control in the five areas we've covered. **In what one or two areas have you exercised a measure of self-control over the past year?**

A _Eating habits, time/health management_

🖐 _Right now, pause and thank God for cultivating within you that degree of self-mastery._

Q **In what one or two areas are you most lacking self-control? (Explain.)**

A _Exercise, spending, thought. life concerning Bob; appropriate conversation around children and to Bob._

Spiritual growth is a mysterious cooperation between you and God. God gives you the capacity to choose, so you aren't passive in the process, but the process itself is never just a matter of fleshly effort. Unless God fills you with His Spirit, traits such as self-control won't materialize. As Watchman Nee said:

> We have spoken of trying and trusting and the difference between the two. Believe me, it is the difference between heaven and hell. It is not something just to be talked over as a good thought; it is stark reality. "Lord, I cannot do it, therefore I will no longer try to do it." This is the point where most of us fail. "Lord, I cannot; therefore I will take my hands off; from now on I trust Thee for that." I refuse to act; I depend on Him to act. It is not passivity; it is a most active life, trusting the Lord like that; drawing life from Him, taking Him to be my very life, letting Him live out His life in me.[14]

versus

As you cease trying to achieve holiness in your own strength and begin by faith to receive the Spirit's power to live a holy life, you will notice a distinct difference. As the fruit of the Spirit is manifested through your life, old sinful habits will begin to drop off one by one. The resulting Christlike character will then radiate to the glory of God the Father.

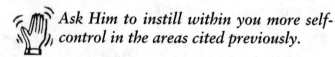 *Ask Him to instill within you more self-control in the areas cited previously.*

Memorizing Scripture

Keeping the fruit of the Holy Spirit in the forefront of your thinking will serve as a constant reminder of God's "character goals" for you. Memorize Galatians 5:22-24 before your study group meets.

"But the fruit of the Spirit is love, joy, peace, patience, kindness, goodness, faithfulness, gentleness and self-control. Against such things there is no law. Those who belong to Christ Jesus have crucified the sinful nature with its passions and desires."

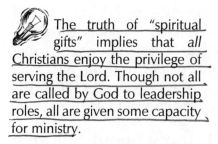The truth of "spiritual gifts" implies that *all* Christians enjoy the privilege of serving the Lord. Though not all are called by God to leadership roles, all are given some capacity for ministry.

How Do I Demonstrate the Gifts of the Holy Spirit?

O n the lawn of most church facilities, you may see a large sign that contains information for the public. A typical sign reads:

Church of the Redeemer
Minister: Alvin Williams

But a rural church in South Carolina had a better idea. After stating their church name, they put their preacher's name beside the term "Pastor." Then the sign read:

Ministers: All the Members!

Although not all believers are called or enabled to be leaders, every follower of Christ is given the responsibility—and privilege—of service. The work of the Holy Spirit is integral to that service. One of the ultimate goals the Spirit has for you is *usefulness*.

The focus of this chapter is another expression of the Spirit's work in your life: *spiritual giftedness*. Just as He yearns to build His character within you, He wants to accomplish His work through you. Through the work of the Holy Spirit *God always equips you for what He calls you to do*.

What Should I Know about Spiritual Gifts?

The Greek word for "gift" means "a capacity or ability that is graciously and freely given." The use of this term points to our unworthiness of such gifts. Because there is nothing in us that deserves such a resource, the initiative lies entirely with the Lord. The word "spiritual" simply refers to the fact that any capacity for service is "caused by the divine Spirit." A gift is nothing we can boast about, since it never originates with us.

It should also be noted that your spiritual giftedness is something completely different and separate from your natural talents, though they may be complementary.

Natural talents, such as musical ability or extraordinary mental capacity, originate with God, whether or not a person acknowledges Him as the source. But Christians must realize that talent is not linked to one's salvation or spiritual state. After conversion a talent may be used in conjunction with a spiritual gift, or it may serve as the avenue for a gift's expression. The talent itself, however, does not ordinarily benefit others in the spiritual

realm apart from the Holy Spirit's activity and the
utilization of a spiritual gift,

Q Summarize the previous two paragraphs *in your own words*. Then write a one-sentence definition of "spiritual gifts."

A Spiritual gifts are the capacity given to a believer through which He uses a person in ministry to others. It is not a talent but may work in connection with a talent. It originates and is activated by Holy Spirit to accomplish his will when a believer surrenders, is filled, and available.

Read the four key New Testament passages on spiritual gifts: Romans 12:3-8, First Corinthians 12:4-27, Ephesians 4:7-16 and First Peter 4:10-11. After digesting the material, answer the following questions.

Q 1. What specific gifts, or capacities for service, can you find in the various passages?

A prophesy, service, teach encourage, giving, leadership mercy, wisdom, knowledge, faith healing, miracles, distinguishing between spirits, tongues, interpretation of tongues, apostleship, evangelism pastoring, speaking

Q Do a comparative study and compile a "master list" of gifts listed in the texts. (Some gifts will be mentioned more than once.)

A

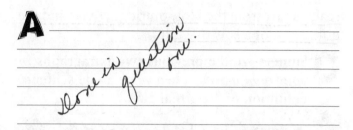

done in question one.

Q 2. Who receives spiritual gifts? (Take phrases directly from God's Word to answer this question.)

A *Each believer, 1 Peter 4:10, each one of us, Eph. 4:7; 1 Corinth 12:7 each one. Roms. 12:6 We have different gifts.*

Q 3. Paul described the church as "the body of Christ." What is the relationship between spiritual giftedness and this analogy?

A *Each gift is a part of the body. All must work together doing their part for the body to be healthy, and fulfill its purpose.*

Q 4. Why does the Spirit allocate spiritual gifts? Find words/phrases from the Bible texts that point to purposes or consequences of believers exercising their gift. (Especially zero in on these verses: First Corinthians 12:7, Ephesians 4:12-16 and First Peter 4:11.)

A *1 Cor. 12:7 → for common good Eph 4:12-16 prepare God's people for works of service, built up Church in unity and maturity reflecting Christ. 1 Pet. 4:11 so God will be praised and glorified.*

Q 5. Mull over the master list of gifts you compiled. What general observations about giftedness and ministry can you make by examining this list?

A _They carry out spiritual application in all aspects of human living; they include all human capacities; inclusive and universal but individually specific_

Q 6. What negative personal attitudes should be eliminated by the truths you've uncovered about spiritual gifts?

A _That one gift is better than another; that some people have a lot while others have none._

What Are My Spiritual Gifts?

Perhaps you think you have a particular spiritual gift, but you aren't sure. That's OK—a lot of believers are in the same boat. Discovering how God has equipped you to serve Him is a process that occurs over time. Try to answer the next few questions based on the experience you've had since conversion.

Q 1. What gift(s) do you feel God has given you?

A _preaching, teaching → exhortation sometimes words of wisdom, Tongues (as prayer language only)_

Q 2. **Why do you think God has enabled you in this way?** (That is, how has the Lord confirmed those gifts?)

A *needs in Body of Christ. mature Christians recognized them. people were spiritually nurtured and/or changed*

Q 3. **In what specific settings or contexts have you exercised the gift(s) you listed previously?**

A *Bible Study leader/teacher Classroom teacher in Dayton Christian High School, pulpit supply, Retreat/ Conference speaker, counseling*

In addition to your personal reflections, take a more objective "Spiritual Gifts Test." Turn to Appendix A at this time and follow the instructions carefully. Be sure to score the test before you return to this page and finish Chapter 11.

Perhaps the following material will also expedite the discovery of your spiritual gifts. In *Unwrap Your Spiritual Gifts,* Ken Gangel offers the following guidelines for recognizing your giftedness:

1. **What do you enjoy doing?** Exercising a spiritual gift should be fulfilling, not burdensome. Christian service has its costs, but it should be a love response to God's faithfulness, not a neurotic, dutiful compulsion.

2. **What ministry effort has God been blessing?** What have you done for the Lord that appar-

ently bore fruit? What observable results have you noticed? Though you won't always see the fruit God brings from your endeavors, over a period of time there should be some indication that your service is not in vain.

3. **How have others encouraged or complimented you?** God often uses friends, family members and teachers to affirm the presence of a particular capacity for service. Especially regard the feedback of mature Christians who suggest a particular ministry for you or point to a particular gift they think you have.

4. **What has the Holy Spirit communicated to you?** God's Spirit confirms your area of giftedness through inner promptings, just as He does your salvation. Ask the Lord to show you how He has equipped you for ministry. He isn't playing hide-and-seek with your spiritual gifts. He wants you to know how and where you can best serve.[1]

We would be remiss if we didn't also mention the importance of *experimentation*, especially regarding skills-oriented gifts such as teaching. Sometimes it's impossible to determine if you have a particular gift until you roll up your sleeves and meet existing needs in people's lives and in church programs. If you are alert to others' needs, areas of spiritual giftedness will emerge from your activity. To put it another way: don't remain passive in the church until you're absolutely sure what your gifts are. In some cases, that would be putting the proverbial cart before the horse! The New Testament teems with commands about work and relationships in the church—mandates for every believer apart from giftedness (such as giving, hospitality, showing mercy and sharing God's Word). If you consistently obey these biblical commands concerning relationships, special capacities for long-term ministry will crystallize.

Questions about Spiritual Gifts

Spiritual giftedness is a controversial, often divisive topic among Christians. Sincere believers disagree on certain facets of the subject. One chapter on spiritual gifts cannot even raise all the issues, much less resolve them. Instead of emphasizing the more controversial aspects of the subject, we've put the spotlight on fundamental truths which almost all believers acknowledge.

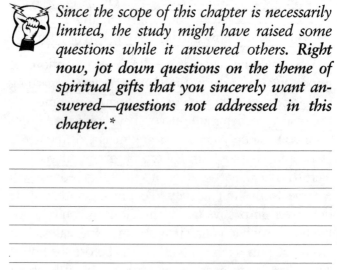 *Since the scope of this chapter is necessarily limited, the study might have raised some questions while it answered others. **Right now, jot down questions on the theme of spiritual gifts that you sincerely want answered—questions not addressed in this chapter.***

_____

_____

_____

_____

_____

_____

*Note: *Appendix B of this book addresses the question of "speaking in tongues."*

Affirming Others' Giftedness

Think of one Christian who has exercised a particular gift in the past (teaching, administration, etc.), but who seems less active for the Lord in recent years or months. This may be a person in your current church or someone you knew years ago. Drop that person a note and inform him of the gift you recognized and the edification that resulted from good stewardship of it. Encourage him to continue using that capacity for service, and not to let it become dormant. *Be sure, however, to keep the tone of your note positive.* (There may be factors you aren't aware of that have caused the person to become less involved in ministry. Your purpose isn't to condemn but to affirm and to stimulate.) *I am that person.*

Consider also this alternative application: Think of a member of your current group whom you're pretty sure has a particular capacity for service. Perhaps you sense that one participant, based on his zeal and ability to express himself, would make a good teacher. Perhaps another has an unusual knack for encouraging others. Or when you divide into smaller groups, perhaps you've noticed that one person in particular keeps the group organized and the discussion on track. Pen a note to this person before the next group meeting. Point out the ministry capacity that you've observed—whether or not you can technically label it a "spiritual gift"—and thank the individual for what he has contributed to the group meetings.[2]

Scripture Memory

By memorizing First Corinthians 12:4-7, you'll never forget the source and purpose of spiritual gifts.

"There are different kind of gifts, but the same Spirit. There are different kinds of service, but the same Lord. There are different kinds of working, but the same God works all of them in all men. Now to each one the manifestation of the Spirit is given for the common good."

> The Christian life is not to be lived in the realm of the natural temperament, and Christian work is not to be done in the power of natural endowment. The Christian life is to be lived in the realm of the Spirit, and Christian work is to be done in the power of the Holy Spirit.[1]
>
> —R.A. Torrey

CHAPTER TWELVE

How Do I Demonstrate the Power of the Holy Spirit?

What do you associate with the phrase, "the power of the Holy Spirit"? Many folks equate the phrase with unusual, supernatural manifestations. They think of miraculous events or some type of eye-popping phenomenon. God *is* capable of the miraculous but even in Scripture miracles were the exception, not the rule. *God's Word associates the "power of the Holy Spirit" not with mind-boggling signs and wonders, but with effectiveness in spreading the gospel.* The dominant evidence of the Spirit's power is usefulness in personal and corporate evangelism. Such usefulness may or may not be accompanied by attention-getting signs.

Notice the link between the Holy Spirit's power and the church's witness in Acts 1:8: "You shall receive power when the Holy Spirit has come upon you; *and you shall be My witnesses* both in Jerusalem, and in all Judea and Samaria, and even to the remotest part of the earth" (emphasis added).

I (Bill) once heard a story about how Alexander the Great conquered the known world of his day. He led armies as far as the Himalayas before he died. After his death, Alexander's generals took a map and spread it before them on a table. They wanted to get a bearing on their location. But their examination of the map astonished them. They couldn't tell where they were, because Alexander had marched them off the best map available in his era.

A mark of any great leader is the ability to take his people farther than they dreamed they could go. A great leader has vision and the competence to help others overcome their fears as they explore new territory. The greatest leader who ever lived—possessor of the most majestic vision of all—was Jesus Christ. His vision for His Church is couched in Mark 16:15: "Go into all the world and preach the gospel to all creation." That's the vision He communicated during His final resurrection appearance, recorded in Acts 1.

Jesus' vision intimidates some people. When it comes to outreach, they feel insecure or inadequate. Rather than marching "off the map" and expanding the borders of the gospel, they prefer familiar territory populated by others who already share their faith. That's why Acts 1:8 is so vital. *To accomplish Jesus' vision is possible—if we're empowered by the Holy Spirit*. According to

A.W. Tozer, "The church must have *power* . . . if she would regain her lost position of spiritual ascendancy and make her message the revolutionizing, conquering thing it once was."[2]

To explore the connection between spiritual power and evangelism in more detail, let's examine the truths in Acts 1:8.

Who Does Christ Want to Use?

Q Look at Acts 1:8 again. **What word represents who it is that Jesus wants to use in spreading the gospel?**

A *the disciples, the eleven and the others with them—believers*

Jesus said "you" shall receive power and "you" shall be witnesses. Of course, the immediate objects of His words were the original disciples gathered around Him just prior to His ascension into heaven. But Christ's commission to penetrate the world with His message is timeless and applies to all His followers. That expectation echoes in Peter's words to believers who were scattered over a wide geographic area: "Sanctify Christ as Lord in your hearts, always being ready to make a defense to everyone who asks you to give an account for the hope that is in you" (1 Peter 3:15).

A witness is someone who communicates to non-Christians the good news of the gospel. In capsule form, here's the content of the gospel:

- *God's purpose:* He created human beings to enjoy a love relationship with Himself.

- *Man's problem:* Because people have chosen sin, their disobedience is a barrier that prevents a relationship with God.

- *God's remedy:* Jesus Christ died on the cross, then was raised from the dead to provide forgiveness for sin, thus bridging the barrier between God and humanity.

- *Man's response:* Whoever places his faith in Christ receives forgiveness and enters into an eternal love relationship with God.

Despite Jesus' mandate and the inherent simplicity of the gospel, only a small percentage of believers share the good news with non-Christians! One reason is that the longer a person knows Christ and participates in a local church, the fewer non-Christians he knows. Research shows that on average the longer a person has been a Christian, the less he engages in personal evangelism. Many long-time Christians grow in their Bible knowledge—perhaps in their character as well—yet they associate less frequently with unchurched people.

 Right now, jot down the names of six non-Christians you know.

Mary   Bill

Bill   Bernarda

Ellen Ann   Kenny

Did you have difficulty writing the names of six *yes!*
non-Christians? If so, <u>God may be nudging you to</u>
<u>cultivate closer relationships with neighbors and</u>
<u>coworkers.</u> If names came readily to mind, <u>view</u>
<u>those relationships as contexts in which you can</u>
<u>express the Holy Spirit's power,</u>

What Is the Scope of the Church's Responsibility?

Jesus' commission to His original disciples in-
cluded an expansive geographic area: ". . . in Jerusalem, and in all Judea and Samaria, and even to the
remotest part of the earth" (Acts 1:8). The power of
the Holy Spirit enables us to win people around the
block, as well as around the world. He obviously
doesn't call most followers to share the gospel in
foreign lands, yet <u>a Spirit-filled person is a "world</u>
<u>Christian" who carries a burden for all unsaved</u>
<u>people</u>. God desires that all men—without distinc-
tion in regard to race, nationality, social status or
economic condition—hear the gospel.

In 1850, approximately 1 billion people populated the earth. The number doubled by 1930. By
1960, the total was 3 billion. By 1975, 4 billion dotted the globe. The population mushroomed to 6 billion by the mid 1990s. To put this evangelistic challenge in perspective, mull over the following facts:
not until the fifteenth century—A.D. 1430—did
Christians represent as much as one percent of the
world's population. It took 360 years (until 1790)
for the proportion of Christians to the world's pop-

ulation to reach two percent. By 1940, Christians accounted for three percent of the populace. Then four percent by 1960; five percent by 1970; six percent by 1980; seven percent by 1983; eight percent by 1986; nine percent by 1989; ten percent by 1993—and eleven percent by 1995. Notice the accelerated rate of evangelistic progress over the past couple of decades. That's cause for encouragement. However, as we move into the twenty-first century, almost ninety percent of the world's 6 billion people are still without Christ. That shows the magnitude of the task that remains.[3]

What Resource Enables Us as Witnesses?

Hurricane Andrew, which destroyed so much of Miami, created some strange phenomena. For instance, one mobile home was so damaged that it lost all but one wall, but on that wall a bulletin board still held children's drawings stuck in with tacks. In another neighborhood tough pine trees were snapped but tender orchids did not lose even a petal. In another location, the winds blew out a living room front window, rear glass doors, destroyed furniture, books, drapes and the television, but left six crystal glasses untouched on a shelf. Mysteries filled one hard-hit home where a fine wall clock, which usually needed winding every other day or so, ticked for more than a week after the storm yet refused to be wound by a key. Then there was a glass lamp that exploded in that same house a week after the hurricane.[4]

To understand how things like this can happen, think about a jet. As long as the plane remains sealed, everything is fine. If you rupture a window, however, the physical laws of nature suddenly demand equilibrium. The more powerful force of outside pressure sucks everything from the inside of the plane. Likewise, during a hurricane, the suction from the pressure change can be so strong that windows or doors are yanked from their frames. Once that happens, the wind gets into the building and can have the same effect as blowing up a balloon.

Wind operates physically in much the same way that the Holy Spirit operates spiritually. Whereas the wind is powerful enough to blow up a house like a balloon, the Holy Spirit is powerful enough to work though men to change the course of history. But, in the same way as a hurricane's winds need a crack in a closed container to create extraordinary effects, so the Holy Spirit needs the believer to provide Him with an opening before He can rush in and create *His* extraordinary effects.

You provide this opening by choosing to trust the Spirit to work though your life as you witness to your non-Christian friends. Consult Acts 1:8. **Underline the words that indicate the resource you need in order to witness effectively.**

Of course, you underlined Luke's reference to the *Holy Spirit*. He wants to infuse you with the burden, the courage and the follow-through that is needed to share your faith. In the same sermon in

which Jesus expressed His desire for His followers
to bear fruit (John 15:16), He explained the integral
role the Holy Spirit would play in their ministries
(14:16, 26; 16:13-14).

That the Holy Spirit's power is integral to outreach was illustrated vividly during Paul's second
missionary journey. Read Acts 16:13-14, which
involves a woman named Lydia and shows the effect of Paul's ministry on her life.

Q What is significant about the remark, "the
Lord opened her heart to respond to the things
spoken by Paul"?

A *It was not Paul or the
preaching: it was the Lord
who opened her heart.*

Like Paul, you're the vessel through whom the
Lord wants to work. You are His <u>mouthpiece</u> but
it is *not* your responsibility to convert others.
<u>Only God's Spirit can open a person's heart and
make him responsive to the gospel.</u>

Q No one responds to a witness unless the Spirit
creates an openness and interest. **What is one
application of our dependence on the Holy
Spirit when we witness?**

*Sensitivity to openness and
interest which comes through
prayer, finding opportunity*

You have learned that evangelism is a dynamic
yet mysterious cooperation between God and His
followers. Only His Spirit can change a human

heart. Nevertheless God has chosen to use His followers as conduits through whom He sends His
powerful message. Before you meet with someone
for the purpose of sharing your faith, pray in-
tently—and ask others to pray for you. Put trust not
in yourself, but in the One who calls you. The
power is in Him, not in you. He will, however, lend
that power to you for the purpose of expanding His
kingdom. A.W. Tozer explains where that power
originates:

> By *power* I mean that divine afflatus which
> moves the heart and persuades the hearer to re-
> pent and believe in Christ. It is not eloquence;
> it is not logic; it is not argument. It is not any of
> these things, though it may accompany any or
> all of them.[5]

Tozer saluted Paul's recognition of the power in
his ministry. Paul's words put a cap on the theme of
this chapter: "My message and my preaching were
not in persuasive words of wisdom, but in demon-
stration of the Spirit and of power, that your faith
would not rest on the wisdom of men, but on the
power of God" (1 Corinthians 2:4-5).

Marching off the Map

You can "march off the map" with Christ by sharing Him with one or more of the six non-Christians
you previously identified. In some instances you
may need to spend time with them and earn the
right to be heard before voicing the gospel. Perhaps
one or more of the persons you named is ready to
hear your witness now.

Ask the Lord to provide the opportunity and the courage to speak to at least one of these non-Christians this week.

Here's an original idea to remind you of these un-saved acquaintances. Purchase a small plant. Tape the names of the six non-Christians to the pot con-taining the plant. Water the plant only after you have prayed for each name that day, or talked to those individuals about spiritual matters. Just as keeping the plant alive requires water, sharing Christ successfully requires prayer and personal ini-tiative.

To facilitate your outreach ministry, study the "One-Verse Method" explained in Appendix C. The One-Verse Method has been used by thousands of ordinary Christians to share the message of salva-tion. This method teaches how to utilize truths in John 3:16 to communicate the gospel.

 After reading through the procedures, practice writing the steps on a blank sheet until you can summarize the method in the space below without referring to Ap-pendix C.

_____

_____

_____

_____

_____

_____

_____

_____

_____

_____

_____

_____

_____

_____

_____

The choice is yours: You can live a life of spiritual poverty or you can live a life of joy and victory. To experience the latter, you must take a risk. You must trust your life to the control of the Spirit of God. Is the risk worth it? Most definitely! Because when you do, <u>He will give you the desire and power to overcome your sinful habits, release your spiritual gift(s) and powerfully share your faith in Christ with non-Christians.</u> It is simply a matter of walking in the Spirit.

Memory Verse

Memorizing Acts 1:8 will solidify within your mind both the responsibility and resource for evangelism.

"But you will receive power when the Holy Spirit comes on you, and you will be my witnesses in Jerusalem, in all Judea, and Samaria and to the ends of the earth."

APPENDIX A

SPIRITUAL GIFTS TEST

Discovering Your Spiritual Gifts

by Dr. Bill Jones

Romans 12:3-9 mentions seven areas of spiritual giftedness. Though this isn't an exhaustive list of the gifts, these seven motivational capacities are considered integral to the life of the church. To discover your dominant motivational gift(s) take the following test. This is by no means an infallible approach to identifying your gifts, but it is a helpful tool that will at least determine areas in which you are motivated to serve the Lord.

Directions:

1. Read through each of the following statements.
2. Answer each one with either "always," "sometimes" or "rarely" using the following numbers to indicate your answer:
   - 2 = Always
   - 1 = Sometimes
   - 0 = Rarely

Test: _____

_2_ 1. I speak God's truth on a subject even when it will not be well received.

_1_ 2. I am often asked to help out in times of special need.

_2_ 3. I enjoy explaining biblical truths.

_2_ 4. I enjoy encouraging others.

_0_ 5. I seek out ministries that need additional material resources.

_0_ 6. I like recruiting others to do work.

_1_ 7. I have a unique understanding of the emotional needs of others.

_2_ 8. I need to communicate God's message verbally.

_2_ 9. I have the ability to find places of ministry that are often overlooked.

_2_ 10. I have a knack for interpreting difficult passages.

_2_ 11. I find myself giving advice to Christians in need.

_1_ 12. I like earning money just to give to God's work.

_2_ 13. I see results in the groups I lead.

_2_ 14. I enjoy visiting people who are sick.

_2_ 15. I feel burdened to speak up when things aren't right.

_1_ 16. I enjoy meeting the physical needs of others.

_2_ 17. I see the need for doctrine to be taught in the church.

_2_ 18. I am able to restore confidence in the discouraged and downtrodden.

_1_ 19. I give generously and joyfully.

_1_ 20. I have the ability to guide people toward group goals.

_2_ 21. I accept those ignored or rejected by others.

_2_ 22. I sense that people feel convicted when I speak.

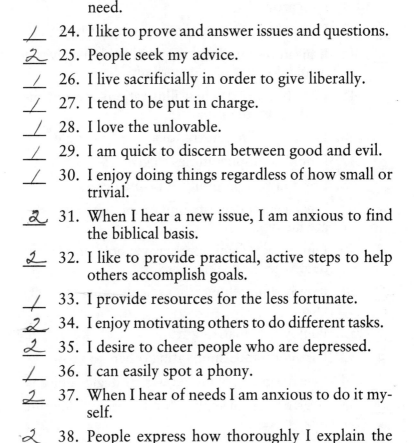

___/___ 23. I concentrate on the practical things others need.

___/___ 24. I like to prove and answer issues and questions.

___2___ 25. People seek my advice.

___/___ 26. I live sacrificially in order to give liberally.

___/___ 27. I tend to be put in charge.

___/___ 28. I love the unlovable.

___/___ 29. I am quick to discern between good and evil.

___/___ 30. I enjoy doing things regardless of how small or trivial.

___2___ 31. When I hear a new issue, I am anxious to find the biblical basis.

___2___ 32. I like to provide practical, active steps to help others accomplish goals.

___/___ 33. I provide resources for the less fortunate.

___2___ 34. I enjoy motivating others to do different tasks.

___2___ 35. I desire to cheer people who are depressed.

___/___ 36. I can easily spot a phony.

___2___ 37. When I hear of needs I am anxious to do it myself.

___2___ 38. People express how thoroughly I explain the Bible.

___2___ 39. I often find myself counseling people.

___/___ 40. When I hear of a need, I immediately think of what I could give.

___/___ 41. I would rather show someone how to do a task than do it myself.

2   42. People who are down respond favorably when I am around.

2   43. I can discern the motives of people's hearts.

1   44. If given responsibility for a fellowship activity I would do most of the work myself.

1   45. I am frustrated when illustrations are not directly from the Bible.

2   46. I often use life illustrations to help people.

0   47. I look for opportunities to give.

2   48. I find myself naturally enjoying people.

2   49. I feel a great deal of compassion for those who are hurting.

2   50. I am direct, frank, persuasive, bold and confident when I speak.

2   51. I enjoy doing things that release others for service.

2   52. I enjoy systematizing truth.

2   53. I am constantly motivating others to grow.

1   54. I see the giving of money as a strategic ministry.

2   55. If given responsibility for a party, I delegate most of it.

2   56. I am painfully aware of another's embarrassment.

1   57. I deeply grieve over the sin I see in society and the church.

2   58. I quickly sense when people need help.

2   59. Definitions of terms are very important to me.

_2_ 60. I want to see people grow and be discipled.

_1_ 61. I get excited about helping financially with a worthwhile project.

_2_ 62. I can sense when a group is spinning its wheels.

_2_ 63. I quickly sense the atmosphere of a group.

_1_ 64. I don't like to compromise.

_2_ 65. I have a hard time saying "no."

_2_ 66. I enjoy spending lots of time in Bible study.

_2_ 67. I think teaching should be practical.

_1_ 68. I am very conscious of my stewardship.

_2_ 69. I am challenged by big goals/long-range plans.

_2_ 70. I am attracted to hurting people.

Scoring:

1. Refer back to the seventy questions above.
2. On page 182, put the number of points (2, 1, 0) in the box corresponding to the question number. (In other words, if you put 2 in the blank for question #1, you would put a 2 in the corresponding box on page 182.)
3. When you have finished, total the points for each column.
4. Graph the total number from each column by finding the appropriate intersection in the graph on page 182 and placing a dot on the line to the right of the category.
5. The highest points on the graph tend to correspond to your strongest motivational spiritual gifts. Note which these are and continue reading the "Developing Spiritual Gifts" section of this appendix.

Prophecy	Serving	Teaching	Exhortation	Giving	Leading	Mercy
1- 2	2- 1	3- 2	4- 2	5- 0	6- 0	7- 1
8- 2	9- 2	10- 2	11- 2	12- 1	13- 2	14- 2
15- 2	16- 1	17- 2	18- 2	19- 1	20- 1	21- 2
22- 2	23- 1	24- 1	25- 2	26- 1	27- 1	28- 1
29- 1	30- 1	31- 2	32- 2	33- 1	34- 2	35- 2
36- 1	37- 2	38- 2	39- 2	40- 1	41- 1	42- 2
43- 2	44- 1	45- 1	46- 2	47- 0	48- 2	49- 2
50- 2	51- 2	52- 2	53- 2	54- 1	55- 2	56- 2
57- 1	58- 2	59- 2	60- 2	61- 1	62- 2	63- 2
64- 1	65- 2	66- 2	67- 2	68- 1	69- 2	70- 2
Total: 16	15	18	20	8	15	18

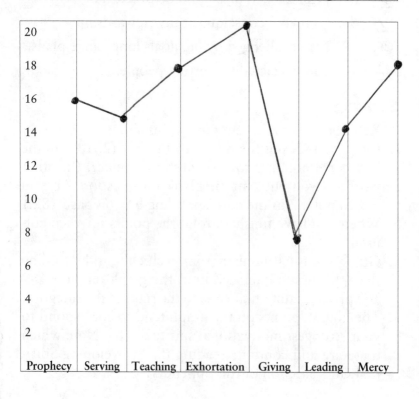

Developing Spiritual Gifts

Now that you have discovered your main spiritual gift (of a motivational nature), you need to develop it to its fullest potential so you can better serve the Body of Christ. One way to do that is to learn the characteristics of your gift so that it can be maximized. Another is to learn how others perceive you so you can avoid any unnecessary complications. Find your primary gift from Romans 12 on the following pages and read your gift's characteristics, complications and cautions. The complications are comments you may hear from other people who don't quite understand your gift or who are helping you become a better steward of your gift. Prayerfully decide which of the cautions you need to put into practice immediately to aid in the development of your gift.

PROPHECY

CHARACTERISTICS
1. Draws sharp lines between good and evil.
2. Holds convictions strongly.
3. Discerning of impure or ungodly motives.
4. Refuses to allow God's standards to be compromised.
5. Hurts deeply over sin (his own and others').
6. Inwardly compelled to speak out on issues of right and wrong.
7. Bold, confident, straightforward, to the point.
8. Desires to see outward results.
9. Presses for change.
10. Frustrated if action is not taken immediately.

COMPLICATIONS
1. "Everything is always 'right' or 'wrong' to you."
2. "You always make mountains out of molehills."

3. "You are judging that person—you suspect the worst of everybody."
4. "Why are you always acting 'holier-than-thou'?"
5. "Get over it; it's not that big of a deal."
6. "You are always poking your nose into other people's business."
7. "You are so insensitive."
8. "Who made you my Holy Spirit, anyway?"
9. "When will you get off my back?"
10. "Nag, nag, nag."

CAUTIONS

1. Learn to ask questions.
2. Consider the spiritual maturity of others.
3. Make sure you are Spirit-led before speaking out.
4. Be firm but not harsh.
5. Be careful not to damage relationships.
6. Do not fear having to stand alone for what is right.
7. Remember you are not the Holy Spirit in another's life.

SERVING

CHARACTERISTICS

1. Sees practical needs that should be met.
2. Puts needs of others ahead of own needs.
3. Wants others' needs to be met quickly.
4. Desires hands-on responsibility.
5. Willing to sacrifice time, effort and money.
6. First to arrive, last to leave (goes the second, third and fourth mile).
7. Seemingly untiring, great stamina.

8. Involved in many activities.
9. More joy over short-term projects than long-range plans.
10. Desires appreciation but not necessarily public recognition.

COMPLICATIONS

1. "Mind your own business!"
2. "You never have time for your family."
3. "We don't want to do it that way."
4. "You are just trying to impress people."
5. "You always do everything yourself. Why don't you let someone else do the work this time?"
6. "You let people take advantage of you."
7. "You are going to burn yourself out."
8. "You can't say 'no' to anyone."
9. "Why didn't you pay attention during the meeting?"
10. "Remember you are serving the Lord, so you shouldn't look to people for appreciation."

CAUTIONS

1. Make sure you are not trying to earn favor or approval (man's or God's).
2. Wait before committing yourself.
3. Realize sometimes it is spiritual to say "no."
4. Pay attention to your devotional life.
5. Take your family into consideration.
6. Live by priorities.
7. Don't overextend yourself; do well what you do; avoid burn out.
8. Don't judge others as lazy or uncommitted too quickly.

TEACHING

CHARACTERISTICS

1. Enjoys studying, researching, learning.
2. Satisfied only by biblical authority.
3. Organizes truth systematically.
4. Fastidious about the definition of terms.
5. Must understand biblical teaching on subject before embracing it.
6. More concerned with what the Bible says than how it applies practically to life.
7. Receives joy from showing others what God's Word says and means.
8. Irritated when Scripture is taken out of context.
9. Wants to know chapter and verse for everything.
10. Dislikes using extra-biblical references as sources of authority.

COMPLICATIONS

1. "Do you do anything besides study the Bible?"
2. "Can't we just carry on a simple conversation without bringing the Bible into it?"
3. "Do you have to make it so complicated? I just want to know what I should do about it."
4. "You get so hung up on 'words.' "
5. "You aren't open enough to the Holy Spirit."
6. "You need to be more practical."
7. "The Bible says this, the Bible says that—quit preaching to me!"
8. "You always find something wrong with his sermons."
9. "Don't get so upset; I know the Bible says it somewhere."

10. "You need to be more open to what you can learn from modern science."

CAUTIONS

1. Worship the God of the Word, not the Word of God.
2. Be sure to make personal applications.
3. Be careful of pride.
4. Don't see knowledge as an end in itself.
5. Don't equate knowledge with maturity.
6. Don't become obsessed with details more than foundational principles (majoring on the minors and minoring on the majors).
7. Be careful of boxing God into your limited understanding.
8. Stay open to the Spirit's leadership.

EXHORTATION

CHARACTERISTICS

1. Needs to see people make progress in spiritual growth.
2. Knows how to help others apply truth.
3. Able to simplify problems by giving people concrete things to do.
4. Enjoys giving others advice or counsel.
5. Understands human nature.
6. Motivates others easily.
7. Likes to use examples from life (theirs or someone else's).
8. Tends to be optimistic about life.
9. Encourages others in words and actions.
10. Frustrated with teaching that is not practical.

COMPLICATIONS

1. "You need to be more patient with him/her."
2. "You talk too much and don't listen enough."
3. "Life isn't always as simple as one, two, three."
4. "Don't lecture me."
5. "You manipulated him."
6. "You just use people."
7. "What I told you was confidential!"
8. "But things are not going OK right now."
9. "Why are you trying to ingratiate yourself?"
10. "People need grounding in doctrine."

CAUTIONS

1. Learn to listen.
2. Be more understanding.
3. Remember God has people on different growth time-tables.
4. Keep confidences.
5. Avoid using people.
6. Don't brag about helping people.
7. Be careful of allowing those who only want someone's attention to dominate your time.

GIVING

CHARACTERISTICS

1. Wisely manages one's resources.
2. Motivated to share; always on the lookout for needs.
3. Wants gift to make a strategic difference.
4. Likes big projects.
5. Needs a relationship with the recipients.
6. Gives sacrificially.

7. Doesn't need a "we're-going-under" appeal to give.
8. Can say "no."
9. Money conscious.
10. Frustrated with wastefulness.

COMPLICATIONS

1. "Why don't you trust God anymore?"
2. "Are you trying to curry favor?"
3. "You have your favorite projects and won't give to anything else."
4. "You can't run the place just because you give so much."
5. "I don't understand why you give to some things and not to others."
6. "You would give away everything we had if I didn't watch you."
7. "You are so tight with your money."
8. "Why are you so selfish?"
9. "You're materialistic. You put too much emphasis on money."
10. "Calm down, we 'needed' it."

CAUTIONS

1. Remember God is the ultimate Source of resources.
2. Pray about your giving.
3. Check the situation with a spouse or parent before giving.
4. Sometimes it is better to give counsel than money.
5. Don't feel badly if you have to say "no."
6. You don't need to impress anyone.
7. Let go of your gift once it is given.
8. Avoid trying to control.

LEADERSHIP

CHARACTERISTICS
1. Sees the big picture.
2. Sets goals.
3. Tends to take charge when no leadership is present.
4. Knows how to organize people and/or programs.
5. Delegates responsibility to others.
6. Uses resources creatively.
7. Tends to be time-conscious.
8. Handles criticism (good or bad) well.
9. Frustrated when things don't run smoothly.
10. Enjoys seeing a plan come together.

COMPLICATIONS
1. "You need to let God work through you."
2. "You care more about projects than people."
3. "You take advantage of people."
4. "You don't appreciate or care about me."
5. "You are so bossy."
6. "You will run over people to accomplish what you want."
7. "You never do any of the work."
8. "You are so callous."
9. "You shouldn't take credit for what God did."

CAUTIONS
1. God is just as concerned with *how* you do something as He is with *what* you do.
2. Remember, in God's economy, people are more important than projects.
3. People work with you, not for you.

4. Be sensitive and tactful when pointing out character flaws or mistakes to your colleagues or to people you supervise.
5. Don't be too hard on people.
6. Express lots of genuine appreciation.
7. Your way is not always the best way.

MERCY

CHARACTERISTICS
1. Compassionate toward the hurting.
2. Unusual ability to sense an atmosphere.
3. Sensitive to others' emotional needs.
4. Attracted to those in distress.
5. Desires to make things better.
6. Establishes heart contact quickly.
7. Shares and empathizes deeply.
8. Wants to help the down-and-out.
9. Patient while another takes time to heal.
10. Frustrated by the insensitivity of others.

COMPLICATIONS
1. "You let others dump on you."
2. "You are always trying to analyze people."
3. "You are being too sensitive."
4. "You let your emotions control you."
5. "You are helping enough hurting people already."
6. "They are focusing more on you than on the Lord."
7. "I feel jealous because you share so deeply with others."
8. "Why are you attracted to someone like that?"
9. "You aren't firm enough."
10. "You shouldn't resent them for not understanding."

CAUTIONS

1. Be led by God's Spirit, not just your emotions.
2. Don't empathize just to get another's attention.
3. Don't allow people to use you.
4. Seek to be discerning.
5. Point them to the Lord, not yourself.
6. Be firm when needed.
7. Be careful around those of the opposite sex.

APPENDIX B

The Question of "Speaking in Tongues"

When topics such as the Holy Spirit and spiritual gifts are discussed, the question of "speaking in tongues" often surfaces. The phenomenon called "speaking in tongues" occurs when a person either prays or speaks in an unknown language, normally unintelligible to persons within earshot. Some Christians believe that "tongues" is evidence of the filling and power of the Holy Spirit. Controversies over this manifestation have driven a wedge between Christians for centuries, resulting in strong opinions that often polarize groups of Christians.

Three basic positions on "speaking in tongues" are common among today's Christians.

1. Some believe that this phenomenon is *the* primary evidence of the Holy Spirit's filling. Every Christian should experience speaking in tongues as evidence of their yieldedness to the Spirit. Persons holding this viewpoint may question the spirituality or commitment of those who do not speak in tongues.
2. Some Christians insist that the Spirit does not distribute the gift of tongues today. They believe the supernatural manifestation of "speaking in tongues" stopped back in the first century. It was a temporary means God employed to authenticate the message and authority of the original apostles. No one who claims to speak in tongues

today does so under the influence of God's
Spirit. Their so-called "gift" is either a psychological manifestation or possibly even demonic
in origin. (You can imagine the discord that
erupts during doctrinal conversations among
persons holding these first two views!)

3. A middle-of-the-road position acknowledges
   that God may still allocate the gift of tongues.
   However, it isn't meant for every Christian,
   nor is it the primary evidence of the Spirit's filling. A Christian does *not* have to speak in
   tongues in order to be "Spirit-filled."

In his discussion on the subject, Paul pointed out
that no one has all the spiritual gifts.

> All are not apostles, are they? All are not proph-
> ets, are they? All are not teachers, are they? All
> are not workers of miracles, are they? All do
> not have gifts of healings, do they? All do not
> speak with tongues, do they? All do not inter-
> pret, do they?" (1 Corinthians 12:29-30)

The Greek construction in Paul's questions demands or assumes a "no" answer. Think of it this
way: your teenager is leaving on a date with un-
kempt hair and a softball-sized hole in his jeans.
You stop him at the door and say, "You aren't going out looking like that, *are you*?" No matter
how the teen responds, it's your conviction that
the appropriate answer is "no."

The third stance on the issue of tongues is our
preference. Who are we to say that God will *never*
bestow this gift on a believer? We are convinced,

however, that the gift of tongues is not something God intends for everyone.

On the Day of Pentecost, some of the disciples spoke in tongues (Acts 2:4). Visitors to Jerusalem who gathered around Jesus' followers heard the gospel proclaimed in their own languages. The gift of tongues to which Paul referred in First Corinthians 12-14 was a different phenomenon. Persons within earshot of someone deploying this gift did not hear the words in a known human language. That's why Paul insisted that any incident of tongues during a church service required the presence of an interpreter—someone with a God-given ability to understand and convey the meaning for everyone present (14:26-28).

Billy Graham wrote, "I am certain about one thing. When the gift of tongues is abused, it becomes divisive and something has gone wrong."[1] Graham elaborated on this subject by offering the following perspective:

- The gift of tongues mentioned in First Corinthians 12-14 is one of the least important gifts in the body of Christ. Paul said that "One who speaks in a tongue edifies himself; but one who prophesies edifies the church" (14:4). He implied that gifts such as teaching eclipse tongues in importance (14:19).

- Tongues is a *gift* of the Holy Spirit, not a *fruit* of the Holy Spirit. Our concern should be on the character that we know

God desires for all Christians (Galatians 5:22-23). God isn't pleased when we're preoccupied with His gifts instead of His character.

- Speaking in tongues is *not necessarily* a sign of the baptism of the believer by the Holy Spirit into the body of Christ, as some believers assert. This is particularly true in the Corinthian context since they had already become part of the body of Christ. No Scripture exists claiming that tongues is a required evidence of the Spirit's baptism of a believer into the church. Nor is tongues a necessary manifestation of the filling of the Spirit. A Christian may spend a lifetime walking in the Spirit's fullness and never speak in tongues.

- The issue of speaking in tongues should be approached sensitively since it is readily abused and open to a variety of interpretations. The fact that Paul devoted most of First Corinthians 14 to the problems it caused in the early church reveals its explosive and controversial nature.

- Pressure by proponents of speaking in tongues has been known to result in counterfeit displays of the phenomenon. Graham tells of a young lady whose close circle of friends all spoke in tongues. She wanted to fit in and find acceptance among them. So she prayed publicly in a known foreign language, which she had acquired while growing up overseas. None of her friends knew that language. She pretended to "speak in tongues" and completely fooled her peers.

- Persons who receive a genuine gift of tongues don't employ it to attract attention, nor do they boast of it to others. Graham knew Corrie Ten Boom, whose story is chronicled in *The Hiding Place*. He said she had experienced the gift of tongues—yet she never publicized that fact or discussed it in a group. She was known to rebuke Christians who persisted in discussing their experience with the gift of tongues.[2]

A.B. Simpson, founder of The Christian and Missionary Alliance, said, "Seek not, forbid not." The Church would do well to heed his wise counsel today. Our best advice is to seek the *Giver* diligently—not particular gifts. God "is a rewarder of those who seek Him" (Hebrews 11:6). Let Him decide whether your rewards include a miraculous gift such as tongues.

Whoever zealously desires to acquire the gift of tongues should instead channel his fervor into service for God. The result will be the fulfillment of the Great Commission and less divisiveness within the church.

APPENDIX C
The One-Verse Method—John 3:16

INTRODUCTION

TRANSITION: Say that John 3:16 is the most famous verse in the entire Bible and that you want to show this person why.

ACTION: Take out a piece of paper and write the words of John 3:16 at the very top of the page in this particular order, leaving room on the page for subsequent steps. (To help you remember this order, note that the middle two phrases both start with the word "that" and both end with a reference to Jesus Christ.) Number these phrases in the following order: 1, 3, 4, 2. (See Step 1.)

John 3:16

1. For God so loved the world,
3. that He gave His only begotten Son,
4. that whoever believes in Him
2. should not perish, but have eternal life.

Step 1: Introduction

EXPLANATION: The reason John 3:16 is so famous is because it summarizes the Bible in four spiritual truths. If you understand these four spiritual truths, you will understand what the entire Bible is all about.

GOD'S PURPOSE

TRANSITION: Let's look at the first truth.

ACTION: Put quotation marks around the words "God," "love," and "world." Then, about halfway down the page, diagram this truth by writing the word "God" on the right, the word "world" on the left, and the word "love" down the middle. (See Step 2.)

John 3:16

1. For "God" so "love"d the "world,"
3. that He gave His only begotten Son,
4. that whoever believes in Him
2. should not perish, but have eternal life.

WORLD   L   GOD
                         O
                         V
                         E

Step 2: God's Purpose

EXPLANATION: God created man to have a personal relationship with Him. He wants this relationship to be one of love, one where God shows His love to people and where people show their love to Him.

TRANSITION: Why do you think that more people are not experiencing this loving personal relationship?

ACTION: Write the word "sin" below the word "love." Then draw two cliffs, one under the word "world," and the other under the word "God." (See Step 3.)

John 3:16

1. For "God" so "love"d the "world,"
3. that He gave His only begotten Son,
4. that whoever believes in Him
2. should not perish, but have eternal life.

WORLD   L   GOD
                         O
                         V
                         E

                        SIN

Step 3

EXPLANATION: It is because of sin. Sin is disobeying God. When someone is offended it causes problems in the relationship. Sin causes a separation between God and man.

MAN'S PROBLEM

TRANSITION: Let's look at the second spiritual truth. It says, "should not perish, but have eternal life."

ACTION: Put quotation marks around the word "perish" and write it under the left-hand cliff, the one with the word "world" on it. Then draw an arrow downward from the word "perish" and write the word "hell." (See Step 4.)

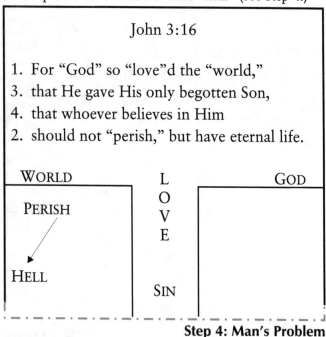

John 3:16

1. For "God" so "love"d the "world,"
3. that He gave His only begotten Son,
4. that whoever believes in Him
2. should not "perish," but have eternal life.

WORLD   L   GOD
      O
 PERISH   V
      E

HELL   SIN

Step 4: Man's Problem

EXPLANATION: It is bad enough to be separated from God and His love, but it gets worse. The Bible says that if anyone dies physically while spiritually separated from God, he will spend eternity in a place called hell.

TRANSITION: That's bad news, but this second spiritual truth also gives some good news.
ACTION: Put quotation marks around the words "eternal life" and write them under the right-hand

cliff. Draw an arrow downward and write the word "heaven." (See Step 5.)

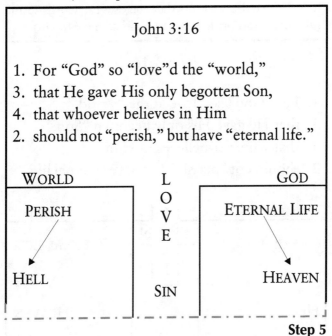

Step 5

EXPLANATION: The good news is that God does not want man to spend eternity in hell. His desire is to have a personal relationship with man so that they can live together forever in a place called heaven.

GOD'S REMEDY

TRANSITION: The question then becomes: How does one deal with his or her problem of sin? That leads us to the third spiritual truth.

ACTION: Put quotation marks around the word "Son" and write it on the diagram so that it shares the "o" in "love." Then draw a cross that encloses the words "Son" and "love" and bridges the two cliffs. (See Step 6.)

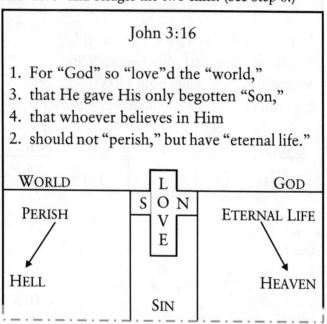

Step 6: God's Remedy

EXPLANATION: God took care of the sin problem by sending His Son, Jesus Christ, to live a perfect life, then die on the cross in order that a person's sin could be forgiven. The amazing thing is that after Jesus was dead and buried, He rose from the dead, proving God has the power to save people from a destiny of torment.

MAN'S RESPONSE

TRANSITION: The question now is, how can a person cross over the bridge that Christ has provided? The fourth spiritual truth gives the answer.

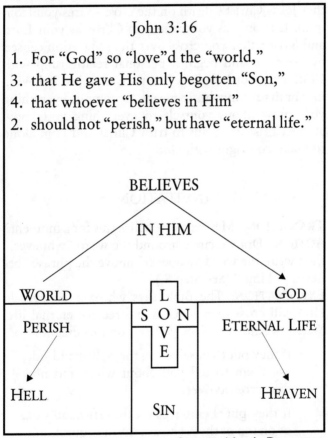

Step 7: Man's Response

ACTION: Draw an arrow from the word "world" to the word "God." Put quotation marks around the words "believes in Him" and write them on top of the arrow. (See Step 7.)

EXPLANATION: It is not enough simply to know (1) that God loves you, (2) that your sin keeps you from that love and will ultimately send you to hell and (3) that Jesus Christ's death on the cross spares you from it all. It is only as you believe in Christ as your Lord and Savior that you cross over the separation caused by your sin and begin a personal relationship with God. This word "believe" is more than just believing in Abraham Lincoln. It means to commit everything you know about yourself to everything you know about Christ. It means to trust Christ and Him alone to make you right with God.

INVITATION

TRANSITION: May we personalize this for a moment?

ACTION: Draw a circle around the word "whoever," then write the word "whoever" above the phrase "believes in Him." (See Step 8.)

EXPLANATION: The Bible says whoever believes in Him will cross over to God and receive eternal life. Where would you place yourself on this diagram?

- If they put themselves on the right-hand side, ask them to tell you about when and how they crossed over.

- If they put themselves on the left-hand side, or on top of the cross, ask the next question.

Do you see anything keeping you from placing your faith in Christ and crossing over to God right now?

If they say "yes," ask them what their questions are and deal with them accordingly. If you do not know the answer to a question, tell them you will try to find out.

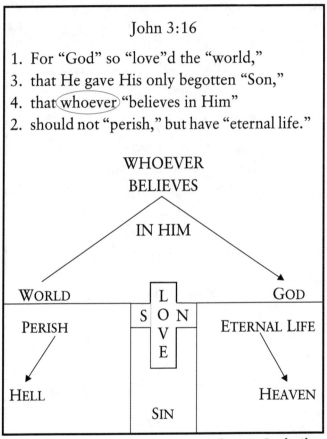

John 3:16

1. For "God" so "love"d the "world,"
3. that He gave His only begotten "Son,"
4. that whoever "believes in Him"
2. should not "perish," but have "eternal life."

WHOEVER
BELIEVES

IN HIM

WORLD   GOD

PERISH   ETERNAL LIFE

HELL   HEAVEN

SIN

Step 8: Invitation

If they say "no," prepare to lead them in prayer expressing their desire to God.

PRAYER OF SALVATION

TRANSITION: If you desire to place your faith in Christ to make you right with God, it's as easy as 1, 2, 3, 4.

ACTION: Put the number 1 under the right-hand cliff, the number 2 under the left-hand cliff, the number 3 under the cross, and the number 4 beside the word "believes." (See Step 9.)

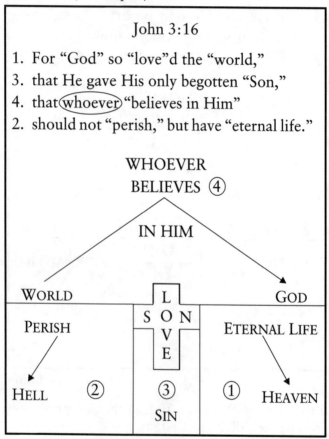

Step 9: Prayer of Salvation

EXPLANATION: If you would like to trust Christ you can do so right now. Tell God: 1) that you are grateful that He loves you; 2) that you are sorry for your sin that has separated you from His love; 3) that you are grateful that He gave His only Son to die on the cross and forgive your sin and 4) that you believe Christ will make you right with Him right now.

I can pray and you can repeat after me. Remember, what is most important is the attitude of your heart, not the words of your mouth. You can pray the right words, but if your heart is not truly convinced that only Christ can make you right with God, then you will not cross over to God. Let's close our eyes and pray right now. (Pray the above four truths back to God.)

PRACTICING John 3:16

Use the space provided on the next page to practice sharing the message of Christ using John 3:16. Do this as much as possible without referring back to the various diagrams. If you must look back, place a smiley face where you got stuck. These smiley faces will serve as a reminder to show where you need to review in order to enhance your presentation.

Follow-Through

1. For practice, present the One-Verse Method using John 3:16 to two people. They can be close friends, family members or others from the discipleship group, if you're going through this book with others.

2. Make notes of what you did best and what needs more work.
3. Look for opportunities to build friendships or talk to non-Christians.

Memory Verse

To expedite your use of the one-verse method, memorize John 3:16.

> For God so loved the world, He gave his only begotten Son that whoever believeth in Him, would not perish but have eternal life.

ENDNOTES

CHAPTER 1 - Who Is the Holy Spirit?

1. Paul Little, *Know What and Why You Believe* (Wheaton, IL: Victor Books, Special edition printed for World Wide Publications, 1980), p. 92.
2. Ibid., p. 55.

CHAPTER 2 - What Does the Holy Spirit Do? (Part 1)

1. Charles Spurgeon, as quoted in Charles Swindoll's *Flying Closer to the Flame* (Dallas, TX: Word Publishers, 1993), p. 263.
2. R.C. Sproul, *Essential Truths of the Christian Faith* (Wheaton, IL: Tyndale House, 1992), pp. 171-172.
3. Billy Graham, *The Holy Spirit* (New York: Warner Books, 1980), p. 55.
4. Watchman Nee, *The Normal Christian Life* (Bombay: Gospel Literature Service, 1957), p. 77.
5. Bill Bright, *The Holy Spirit: The Key to Supernatural Living* (San Bernadino, CA: Here's Life Publishers, 1980), p. 15.
6. Charles Stanley, *The Wonderful Spirit-Filled Life* (Nashville, TN: Thomas Nelson, 1992), p. 33.
7. Bright, p. 15.
8. Merrill Unger, *The Baptism and the Gifts of the Holy Spirit* (Chicago: Moody Press, 1974), p. 21.

CHAPTER 3 - What Does the Holy Spirit Do? (Part 2)

1. Terry Powell, *Welcome to the Church* (Littleton, CO: LAMP, 1987), p. 34.
2. Michael Green, ed. *Illustrations for Biblical Preaching* (Grand Rapids, MI: Baker Book House, 1989), p. 190.

CHAPTER 4 - Why Am I Not Experiencing the Holy Spirit's Power?

1. Vance Havner, *Pepper and Salt* (Grand Rapids, MI: Baker Book House, 1966), p. 9.
2. Bright, p. 6.
3. Robertson C. McQuilkin, *Joy and Victory* (Chicago: Moody Press, 1953), p. 46.
4. Andrew Murray, *The Full Blessing of Pentecost* (Fort Washington, PA: Christian Literature Crusade, 1954), pp. 40-46.
5. A.W. Tozer, *The Pursuit of Man* (Camp Hill, PA: Christian Publications, 1978), p. 137.
6. Graham, p. 159.
7. Ibid., p. 131.
8. Jerry Bridges, *The Pursuit of Holiness* (Colorado Springs, CO: NavPress, 1978), p. 84.
9. Ruth Paxson, as quoted by Jack Taylor in *The Key to Triumphant Living* (Nashville, TN: Broadman Press, 1971), p. 31.
10. Adapted from Hannah Smith's *The Christian's Secret of the Happy Life* (New York: Fleming H. Revell, 1941), p. 38.
11. Billy Graham, quoting Ruth Paxson, p. 187.

CHAPTER 5 - How Do I Grieve the Holy Spirit?

1. Graham, p. 186.
2. Bright, p. 52.
3. Graham, p. 131.
4. Kenneth Wuest, *Word Studies in the Greek New Testament*, vol. 1 (Grand Rapids, MI: Eerdmans, 1973), p. 157.
5. *Webster's New World Dictionary of the American Language*. Second college edition. (Cleveland, OH: William Collins and World Publishing, 1976), p. 1359.
6. Wuest, p. 158.

7. Graham, pp. 188-189.

8. Wuest, p. 101.

CHAPTER 6 - How Do I Quench the Holy Spirit?

1. Green, p. 191.

2. Bright, p. 65.

3. Ibid., p. 52.

4. James McConkey, *The Three-Fold Secret of the Holy Spirit* (Chicago: Moody Press, 1987), p. 68.

5. Jerry Adler, "Blow Up," *Newsweek*, July 18, 1984, pp. 28-31.

6. Graham, p. 191.

7. George Mueller, as quoted in Graham's *The Holy Spirit*, p. 69.

8. Swindoll, pp. 135-137.

9. Ibid., pp. 133, 150.

10. John Piper, *A Hunger for God* (Wheaton, IL: Crossway Books, 1997), pp. 113-114.

11. Andrew Murray, *The New Life* (Minneapolis, MN: Bethany Fellowship, 1965), p. 112.

12. Adapted from material received from Pastor Peter Lord of Florida.

CHAPTER 7 - What Does It Mean to Be "Filled with the Holy Spirit"?

1. From an April 1972 chapel message delivered at Wheaton College by Stuart Briscoe.

2. Roy Hession, *Be Filled Now* (Fort Washington, PA: Christian Literature Crusade, 1967), p. 12.

3. R.A. Torrey, as quoted by Charles Stanley in *The Wonderful Spirit-Filled Life*, p. 34.

4. Sharon Begley, "The Second Wind," *Newsweek*, CXX, No. 4, July 27, 1992, p. 59.

5. Swindoll, p. 84.

6. Ibid., p. 83.

7. Jack Taylor, *The Key to Triumphant Living* (Nashville, TN: Broadman, 1971), p. 83.

8. Swindoll, pp. 75, 78.

CHAPTER 8 - How Can I Be Filled with the Holy Spirit?

1. Little, p. 99.

2. Richard Foster, *Celebration of Discipline* (San Francisco, CA: Harper & Row, 1978), p. 6.

3. Taylor, p. 93.

4. Murray, *The Full Blessing of Pentecost*, p. 53.

5. Hannah Smith, *The Christian's Secret of a Happy Life* (New York: Fleming H. Revell, 1941), p. 48.

6. Taylor, p. 95.

7. McConkey, pp. 51-52.

8. Nee, p. 97.

9. Murray, *The Full Blessing of Pentecost*, p. 64.

10. McQuilkin, p. 50.

11. Taylor, p. 96.

12. Smith, p. 47.

13. McConkey, p. 68.

14. Charles S. Trumbull, *Victory in Christ* (Fort Washington, PA: Christian Literature Crusade, 1992), p. 14.

15. Robert Witty, *Power for the Church* (Jacksonville, FL: Pioneer Press, 1966), p. 57.

16. Graham, p. 148.

17. Swindoll, p. 81.

18. Trumbull, p. 32.

CHAPTER 9 - How Can I Walk in the Holy Spirit?

1. Swindoll, p. 81.

2. Bridges, p. 58.

3. Murray, *The New Life*, p. 122.

4. This anecdote was inspired by material from Bill Bright's *The Holy Spirit*, p. 131.

5. Bright, p. 46.

6. Ibid., p. 47.

7. Little, p. 99.

8. Neil Anderson, *Victory Over the Darkness* (Ventura, CA: Regal Books, 1990), p. 97.

CHAPTER 10 - How Can I Exhibit the Fruit of the Holy Spirit?

1. Eugene Peterson, *A Long Obedience in the Same Direction: Discipleship in an Instant Society* (Downers Grove, IL: InterVarsity Press, 1980), p. 12.

2. Adapted from "Stories Behind Six Popular Christian Hymns," in *Worldwide Challenge*, March/April, 1985, p. 10.

3. Horatio G. Spafford, "It Is Well with My Soul," *Hymns of the Christian Life* (Camp Hill, PA: Christian Publications, 1978), # 300.

4. J. Stephen Lavey, "Pillar Sitters, Penitents, and Pilgrims," *Discipleship Journal*, Issue 49, 1989, p. 35.

5. Source unknown.

6. From an April 1972 chapel message delivered at Wheaton College by Stuart Briscoe.

7. Charles H. Spurgeon, as quoted in Billy Graham's *The Holy Spirit*, p. 287.

8. V. Raymond Edman, *The Disciplines of Life* (Wheaton, IL: Victor Books, 1948), p. 80.

9. Bright, p. 161.

10. Ibid., p. 163.

11. Charles Swindoll, *Improving Your Serve* (Waco, TX: Word Books, 1981), p. 105.

12. Adapted from Jerry Bridges' *The Pursuit of Holiness*, p. 118.

13. John MacArthur, "Mastery of Materialism," as quoted by Ron Blue in "Money—If God Owns It All, What Are You Doing with It?" *Discipleship Journal*, Issue 53, 1989, p. 22.

14. Nee, p. 101.

CHAPTER 11 - How Do I Demonstrate the Gifts of the Holy Spirit?

1. Adapted from Kenneth Gangel, *Unwrap Your Spiritual Gifts* (Wheaton, IL: Victor Books, 1983), pp. 13-14.

2. The application exercises for Chapter 11 are adapted from Terry Powell's *Welcome to Your Ministry: Study Guide* (Littleton, CO: Lay Action Ministry Program, 1985), p. 46.

CHAPTER 12 - How Do I Demonstrate the Power of the Holy Spirit?

1. R.A. Torrey, *How to Find Fullness of Power in Christian Life and Service* (Minneapolis, MN: Dimension Books [Bethany Fellowship]). Reprinted from 1903 edition of James Nisbet & Co. of London, n.d.), pp. 77-78.

2. A.W. Tozer, *Paths to Power* (Camp Hill, PA: Christian Publications, 1964), p. 9.

3. Evangelistic challenge statistics provided by the U.S. Center for World Missions, as cited in Bill Jones' "Mastering Evangelism" notebook, published by Crossover Communications International.

4. Source unknown.

5. Tozer, *Paths to Power*, p. 13.

APPENDIX B - The Question of "Speaking in Tongues"

1. Graham, p. 250.

2. Adapted and expanded from Graham, pp. 256-264.

MEMORY VERSES

Chapter 1 John 14:16-17
Chapter 2 John 7:37-39
Chapter 3 Luke 4:1, 14
Chapter 4 Galatians 5:19-21
Chapter 5 Ephesians 4:30
Chapter 6 First Thessalonians 5:19
Chapter 7 Ephesians 5:18
Chapter 8 Luke 11:13
Chapter 9 Galatians 5:16-18
Chapter 10 Galatians 5:22-24
Chapter 11 First Corinthians 12:4-7
Chapter 12 Acts 1:8

Bill Jones is president of Crossover Communications International. Crossover is a missions organization helping to fulfill the Great Commission in Eurasia, currently focusing on the countries in the area of the Black Sea. Bill also serves as the program director for the Master of Arts in Missions and the Master of Arts in Leadership at Columbia International University in Columbia, South Carolina. A passionate communicator, Bill has trained thousands of people all around the world to effectively share their faith in Christ.

Terry Powell has a Ph.D. in Education Ministry from Trinity Evangelical Divinity School and teaches Christian Education and Bible at Columbia International University.

CROSSOVER
COMMUNICATIONS
INTERNATIONAL

P.O. Box 211755   Columbia, SC 29221
Phone: (803) 691-0688   Fax: (803) 691-9355
www.crossoverusa.org

Write to Terry Powell or Bill Jones at:
CIU
P.O. Box 3122
Columbia, SC 29230
or call (803) 754-4100